The Naked Truth

**Everything You've Always Wanted to Know
About the IRS but Couldn't Afford to Ask**

163 Questions and Indepth Answers
About the Internal Revenue Service

by Daniel J. Pilla

WINNING Publications
St. Paul, Minnesota

WINNING Publications
506 Kenny Road
St. Paul, Minnesota

Copyright © 1986 by Daniel J. Pilla

All rights reserved. No portion of this book may be reproduced in any form, except quotations for purpose of review, with full credit given. Quotations from this book for any other purpose must be authorized in writing by the author.

First Edition, August, 1986

Printed in the United States of America.

Library of Congress Catalog Card Number 86-90235

ISBN: 0-9617124-0-6

Notice from the Author and Publisher

This book is designed to provide the author's findings and opinions based on research, analysis and experience with the subject matter covered. This information is not provided for purposes of rendering legal, accounting or other professional advice. It is intended purely for educational purposes.

The author and publisher disclaim any responsibility for any liability or loss incurred as a consequence of the use and application, either directly or indirectly, of any information presented herein.

Because the United States currently functions under an evolutionary legal system, the reader bears the burden of assuring that the principles of law stated in this work are current and binding at the time of any intended use or application. Caution: The law in this country is subject to change arbitrarily and without prior notice.

Dedication

To Bob and Chuck, two men whose understanding of righteous judgment is unsurpassed by any other persons I have ever known.

Acknowledgments

The author wishes to thank those close to him for their helpful guidance in developing this work: my brother Joe for endlessly encouraging it; Jerry Peterson for his masterful cover painting; Mike Culbert for his expert editorial analysis of the manuscript; my father for pulling together the final printing; and my wife, Jeanne, for her patience, support and understanding.

Special Acknowledgment

It is not very often that life's outrageous fortunes make it possible to meet a person whose history, spirituality and purposes seem to so closely parallel one's own that, but for names and places, they might just as well be the same. To meet such a person is a great benefit, for when the efforts of both are dedicated to the accomplishment of a common goal, synergism in the purest sense of the word is achieved. Such a relationship has manifested itself in my life in the person of David Engstrom. Three years ago, we began work on a project which was never to be. As it turned out, that apparent failure was no failure at all, but rather was the first chapter in what was to become a voluminous ledger of success. This book is but the first plateau of the mountain upon whose conquest we have embarked. There is more to come. Daves objective judgment and sound insight into the nature of humankind will, more than any other single factor, mean the difference between the ultimate success or failure of this and our future efforts. Without his work, this manuscript would still be just one more thing I knew I should do if I ever got the time.

"Experience should teach us to be most on our guard to protect liberty when the Government's purposes are beneficent. Men born to freedom are naturally alert to repel invasion of their liberty by evil-minded rulers. The greatest dangers to liberty lurk in insidious encroachments by men of zeal, well-meaning but without understanding."

Supreme Court Justice Louis Brandeis
Olmstead v. United States, (1928)

Table of Contents

Introduction	**7-24**
Chronological List of Questions Answered	**25-36**
Preview to this Work	**37**
Chapter One - The Knock on the Door Questions Relating to Audit	**38-81**
Chapter Two - Avenues of Hope Questions Relating to Appeals	**82-104**
Chapter Three - Your Worst Fears Questions Relating to Collection	**105-143**
Chapter Four - Under the Gun Questions Relating to Criminal Investigation	**144-175**
Chapter Five - Untangling the IRS Miscellaneous Questions	**176-192**
Chapter Six - Whither America? The Ultimate Question	**193-208**
Table of Abbreviations	**209**
Bibliography	**210-211**
Information Tear-Out Sheet	**212**
About the Author	**213**

INTRODUCTION

Have you ever feared something you didn't understand? If you have, then you know that a lack of understanding can be very expensive, in more ways than one. If you have experienced the kind of fear brought on by ignorance, then you also realize that once the ignorance is cured the fear is usually exposed as totally groundless.

It is this very fact that has kept Americans glued to the movie and television screens for years watching horror and suspense films. One such film I recall is a made-for-television episode of Sherlock Holmes shot in the late 1940's. In the production, Holmes is called to the French town of La Ma Rouge to investigate a murder and the inhabiting of the local marsh by an apparent ghost.

The ghost has the townspeople terrified. Those who have seen it — something definitely does exist — describe it as a glowing human figure which moves swiftly through the marsh. Of course, nobody wants to get close enough to see what it actually is as all are aghast at the thought of coming into direct contact with it.

When a murder occurs, local authorities are convinced that the apparition is somehow responsible but are powerless — by reason of fear — to do anything about it. Enter Sherlock Holmes with his inimitable skill of deductive reasoning. After an investigation consisting chiefly of observation of the tiniest details, Holmes exposes the apparition for what it is — a man wearing clothing treated with phosphorus to make it glow in the dark. His treks through the marsh while dressed in the eery garb were designed to induce fear in the townspeople so as to keep them from preventing the murder he planned, or connecting him with it once carried out.

The scheme was successful until Holmes exposed it. Having done so, the local authorities kicked themselves for not discovering it on their own. After all, once explained, Holmes' use of deductions and logic was childishly simple.

In nearly every area of our lives, we come across circumstances akin to the La Ma Rouge apparition, if not in form, surely in substance. Personal ignorance leads to fear which in turn fosters inaction. The result is that we are in some way taken advantage of.

8 INTRODUCTION

This is especially true with the Internal Revenue Service. That seemingly all-powerful federal agency is surrounded in ambiguity and we have all heard horror stories which help to create and proliferate fear. We know that IRS audits millions of tax returns every year and the biggest fear we have is that ours will be among those selected. The result is that we are taken advantage of by the agency, or, worse, we allow ourselves to be intimidated to the point where we do not assert our rights to their fullest legal potential.

A classic example of this is when a person boasts that after his audit he was given a refund by the IRS. The reason, he contends, is that in anticipation of a possible audit, he didn't claim all that he was entitled to at the time of filing his return. Actually, what the IRS has done is to push this person into a position where, out of fear of audit and its unknown ramifications, he doesn't claim all the deductions the law entitles him to. And although he did receive a refund for the one year in which he was audited, he will never get a refund for the years in which he is not audited. Ultimately, he is deprived of money which is lawfully his all because he was intimidated by the thought of an audit.

Over the years, this fear and ignorance has grown into a quiet hysteria, the kind of fear that sweeps over a person who, while lying in bed, hears the sound of his own front door slowly opening. Unfortunately, this fear is not completely unfounded. It is well known that the IRS has powers which no other federal agency has. We have all heard or read of horror stories which seem to have as their central theme the fact that the IRS has destroyed the lives of innocent citizens, sometimes in a dispute over just a few dollars.

In addition, agents of the IRS have awesome powers, which, in many cases are unchecked by supervisory personnel. For example, Revenue Officers have the power to seize assets and levy wages, in many cases, without any prior approval of higher-ups, much less the federal courts. As if this were not enough, federal laws make it nearly impossible to stop the IRS in the collection of taxes, even if they are dead wrong on the issue. But the power doesn't end there, it goes on. For example, this most singular agency is the only federal agency which can:

INTRODUCTION 9

— estimate your yearly income and bill you for tax based upon that estimate;[1]

— gain access to your bank records without a court order;[2]

— force you to turn over your personal records and give testimony about yourself on an annual basis (the IRS audit);[3]

— seize your paycheck without a court order and force you to support yourself and family on the grand total of $75.00 per week;[4]

— confiscate your Social Security or pension, even if it's your only source of income;[5]

— sell your personal homestead residence;[6]

— force you into a position where you must prove your innocence rather than the conventional American standard which holds that you are innocent until proven guilty.[7]

Yes, the IRS does have awesome power to audit tax returns, create tax liabilities and enforce collection of income taxes. And given the present level of awareness by the American people as to those powers and their limitations, it's no wonder that people are afraid and are taken advantage of by the mammoth agency.

While people are intellectually aware of these facts and the problems that go with them, they don't seem emotionally to accept them; it's the difference between hearing and listening. You know that the IRS audits millions of people every year, but you take comfort in the shallow notion that it won't happen to you. Or you try to placate yourself by believing that because you have all your records, no harm can befall you.

Records or no records, the fact is that the threat of an IRS audit is one of the single most terrifying ideas to the typical U.S. citizen. Why? Because the average American does not know what happens during an audit. He doesn't know what happens after an audit should he be sent a bill. And, the most terrifying unknown is he doesn't know why he was selected

---

[1] 26 USC §6020(b). All statutory references in this work are to the Internal Revenue Code of 1954 as amended, unless otherwise indicated.
[2] 26 USC §7609.
[3] 26 USC §7602.
[4] 26 USC §§6331 and 6334.
[5] 26 USC §6334.
[6] **United States v. Rogers**, 461 U.S. 677 (1983).
[7] **Hevlering v. Taylor**, 296 U.S. 507 (1935).

10 INTRODUCTION

for an audit. Was it something he claimed on the return? Or more probably, was it something he didn't claim on the return? What should or shouldn't he say during the audit? Who can help? What will it cost? Have I done anything wrong? What can they do? What are my rights?

These questions and countless others overrun the minds of those with even the most copious records as would the lights and bells of a pin ball machine. The sad reality is, whether you admit it or not, Americans are at the mercy of the IRS and the agency knows it.

Worse yet, all indications from within the agency itself are that this situation will not dissipate in the coming years. Indeed, IRS has published documents which indicate, in no uncertain terms, that they intend to step-up their involvement in our lives. They intend, they say, to develop and maintain a sense of "presence" through regular audits of all taxpayers, and through increased computer contacts, and by targeting specific segments of society for intensified investigatory activity, and by involving other agencies of government — both state and federal — in the tax collection process. The bottom line is this: You **will** be audited.

On May 9, 1984, the IRS issued document number 6941 entitled **Internal Revenue Service Strategic Plan.** The Plan, not unlike that which would be drawn by the commander-in-chief of an army about to invade a foreign land, details the programs the IRS will initiate in the next several years in an effort to make the job of collecting taxes more "profitable and efficient." In the Plan, Roscoe L. Egger, Jr., then Commissioner' of the Internal Revenue Service, makes this statement:

> "It is with a sense of considerable pride that I approve the Strategic Plan to carry out the Mission of the Service. The Plan consists of the Statement of Strategic Direction and the fifty-five initiatives to translate them into action. It is the product of a tremendous team effort by a large group of Service executives. Clearly without their effort and commitment we could not have achieved these results.
>
> This Plan provides a strong foundation for directing tax administration efforts well into the 1990s and lays the groundwork for the Service's entry into the 21st century. Approval, however, is only the beginning. Still ahead are

the major tasks of effectively implementing the approved initiatives and keeping the Plan current."

Mr. Egger talks of a "Mission," "Strategic Direction" and "initiatives" as though he were a battlefield general rather than the chief United States tax collector. In the subsequent 204 pages, one finds the specific details of the plan Mr. Egger so warmly welcomes into the fold of bureaucratic reality.

Not surprisingly, one area keenly focused upon is that of technology and automation. After reading the report we find that the IRS has and will continue to upgrade its computer system at a cost to the taxpayer of nearly 100 million dollars. What will this enhanced high-tech power enable the IRS to accomplish? Mr. Egger provides the answer:

> "Automation continues to redirect the tax administration world and redefine the way we collect the nation's revenues. Beyond individual automation efforts, the overall dimensions of a totally redesigned tax system are beginning to take shape. Within the next five to 10 years, we will have a totally redesigned tax administration system. Paper tax returns can largely be a thing of the past. And tax processing procedures that now take weeks and months will be reduced dramatically.
>
> **"We do not have to wait for the future to see tremendous change. Consider some of the things that happened just last year:**
>
> **"Automated Collection.** We saw the last of the 21 automated collection sites come on-line. . .Beyond the staff saving, early indications are that the automated system enables us not only to collect more efficiently but to collect more dollars in less time.
>
> **"Automated Exam.** This year we set in motion a three-step plan to automate the examination process. First there will be an analysis of our current system and a new system design. The second phase will put computer terminals and software in the hands of all revenue agents by the fall of 1985 to help compute tax on the spot, write reports and do technical research.***
>
> **"Optical Scanning.** Optical character recognition equipment now reads federal tax deposit cards and our simplest tax form, the 1040 EZ. Our next hurdle will be a system-wide scanning of paper information returns.

And we are adding other new tax processing applications all the time.***

The Service, Egger seems to be saying, is to be streamlined through automation. He foresees streamlined audits, streamlined collections, streamlined investigations — the ability to do more with less, to extend the reach of the IRS — a reach some say has already gone too far.

In years past, the IRS audit and investigation processes were slow and cumbersome, if no less intrusive. Congressional investigations revealed the kind of "old-fashioned" leg work the IRS once used to carry out its vigilance.

Ten years ago, Senator Frank Church of Idaho conducted hearings on the domestic intelligence activities of the IRS — that is, their acts of spying on the citizens of the United States. During these hearings before the **Select Committee to Study Governmental Operations with respect to Intelligence Activities**, it came to light that the IRS maintained a "hit list" developed to audit, harass and intimidate some 8000 individuals and 3000 organizations "though clearly from the nature of these organizations, they (were) not suspected of owing taxes."

Among the groups targeted were The Congress of Racial Equality, The Medical Committee for Human Rights, Church League of America, Free Speech Movement, Institute for American Democracy, Inc., The Peace Foundation, The American Jewish Congress, Associated Catholic Charities, The American Law Institute, and the U.S. Civil Rights Commission.

The hearings ended with the finding that:

". . .what your testimony shows[8] is that, at least as of now, every taxpayer in this country is on notice that when his tax return is filed in the IRS, it means any agency in the Government that can claim an official interest can get into that tax return for its own purposes. That is what it means. **And, what better form is there to intimidate people, harass people, force them to comply with whatever it is some other agency may have in mind, than to have his tax return and information that it may contain.**" (Emphasis added.)

---

[8] Senator Church is referring to the testimony of then Commissioner of Internal Revenue Donald C. Alexander.

INTRODUCTION 13

The Committee report was shocking. It exposed the fact that IRS routinely engaged in undercover surveillance of public meetings, regularly used "undercover operatives" to "supply contacts" with statements made by citizens under investigation, and used "some old-fashioned bird-dogging; that is, the taking of license numbers of the most expensive looking automobiles" present at public gatherings to develop lists of people to audit.

Perhaps the most bizarre revelation coming from the hearings was the fact that the FBI and even the CIA regularly asked for **and were given** the tax returns of any person or organization it wished.

You might be inclined to say, though these circumstances were clearly abusive, they happened 10 years ago and don't happen any more. Perhaps blind faith and naivete" would suggest a positive reaction to this argument. The facts, however, present an entirely different picture. The portrait of enhanced technological capabilities painted by the Plan seems to indicate that the IRS can carry on their surveillance activities without going to the trouble of "old-fashioned bird-dogging." They can now use a new and modern form of "bird-dogging" by optically scanning paper information returns.

Furthermore, evidence suggests that the old hit lists compiled for purposes clearly unrelated to income taxation are still in existence, but are now of a more high-tech character. The "hit lists" are now compiled on the basis of compliance "soft spots" or on the basis of the members' ability to provide "leads" for use in examinations.

The IRS' incredible computer power enables them to cull out persons from the general list of taxpayers for placement on a separate, "soft spot" list. The names are then given further attention in the form of computer contacts and actual audits. The taking of license numbers may be a thing of the past, but the end result is still the same: First — contact in writing, then, an audit.

To this end, the Plan labels the self-employed person as a "traditional 'soft spot' in our otherwise good compliance" system, since self-employed persons can more easily "escape the 'safety-net'" of the IRS' watchful eye. More specifically, the IRS now has singled out direct marketing self-employeds such as Amway or Shaklee distributors, apparently due to

14   INTRODUCTION

"schemes used by part-time Amway distributors on their individual returns throughout the country." The Plan calls for the regular audit and examination of all self-employeds. They will be the first group subjected to regular audit under the new guidelines.

What's more, a list of fruitful "sources of tax evaders" has been compiled for use by agents during their audits. The list includes men's and women's clothing shops, furriers, jewelers, antique shops, travel agencies, exclusive clubs, exclusive furniture stores and interior decorators. These businesses have been singled out for audit because IRS believes they may discover "leads indicating possible tax evasion by taxpayers doing business with (those) firm(s)."

There can be no argument that the use of technology in this fashion places incredible power in the hands of the IRS — power to actually see and, hence, control every aspect of one's private life. As if this is not enough, consider the statement Egger makes that within five to ten years "paper tax returns can largely be a thing of the past." If IRS doesn't need a tax return from you any longer, then it's reasonable to assume that they will already have the information needed to compute your tax liability. But how will they come into possession of the necessary data if you didn't supply it and they aren't doing any "old-fashioned bird-dogging"?

Perhaps the key to the enigma lies in Egger's suggestion that IRS intends a "system-wide" application of optical scanning equipment to read "paper information returns." Optical scanning equipment is nothing more than a computer with eyes that can literally read and imput data from a sheet of paper. Information returns are filed by the hundreds of millions every year reporting virtually every transaction. They include Forms W-2, which report wages, and 1099, which report interest and other earnings. No longer will it be necessary for a person to physically key-punch the data from those information returns into the computer banks.

Optical scanning equipment **could** make "paper tax returns. . .a thing of the past." But to do so effectively, every wholesale, retail and service organization in America would have to report to the IRS on a specially designed information return what they sold, when, to whom and for how much. This information could then be optically fed into the central computer and maintained by Social Security number, which would also have to be shown on the new form. Small businesses would probably have to prepare and file the forms by hand, on paper, while large firms could file them on magnetic tape as they now do with payroll records.

At the end of the year, IRS could compute your tax liability since they would have all your financial data in their computer. All you'd have to do is pay the bill you receive in the mail. Is this the kind of "paperless tax return" Egger is dreaming of? If so, IRS has come full circle in the gathering and maintenance of personal information.

If this kind of futuristic progress is indeed that which Egger foresees, consider the Orwellian-like[9] impact such a system would have on your life. Since all purchases would have to be accompanied with a Social Security number, you wouldn't be able to transact any business without such a number, as it represents your name. And, since your earnings are reported under your Social Security Number, your income and disbursements could easily be seen by simply punching up your number. Hard to imagine? Keep in mind that Egger hopes to have "computer terminals and software in the hands of all revenue agents by the fall of 1985 to help compute tax **on the spot**, write reports and do technical research." (Emphasis added.)

With this kind of ability, any given IRS agent could punch-up your computer ledger, and, for example, see that your yearly income was $22,500, and that you purchased a $1,750 sailboat. He could then check the sophisticated statistical records kept by IRS to find that a $1,750 sailboat can only be supported by somebody earning $26,800 per year.

Behold, the computer has discovered a discrepancy! You've purchased more than your **apparent** income can support. Are you receiving unreported income? Possibly from an illegal source? Only a full scale audit will reveal the truth. You are called in and the agonizing process begins.

The Church hearings indicated that the IRS was compiling lists for use by other governmental agencies. The Plan, ten years later, implores other agencies of government to make lists for the IRS, presumably to enhance the efficacy of the paperless return system. The Plan calls for the IRS to:

---

[9] See George Orwell's book **1984**, a fictional account of the nature and character of government by the year 1984. The book was written in 1948.

16   INTRODUCTION

> "Establish a multifunctional task force to compile an index of investigatory activities conducted by other federal Government agencies that may be beneficial to the IRS.*** In some cases it may be possible to execute Interagency Agreements which would facilitate the securing of information."

Among the steps to be taken in this area is the promotion of state legislation which would require that:

> "1) any person providing goods or services to, or real estate space for, the state or any subdivision thereof, and 2) any person applying to the state, or any subdivision thereof, for a right or license, or renewal thereof, to conduct a profession, trade, or business within the state. . .to establish or certify under penalty of perjury that the person has filed all return(s) and paid any tax required by the State."

The purpose of this kind of legislation, according to the Plan, is "to surface delinquent or nonfiler taxpayers through matching the 'certifications' with the state's income tax records. The state's income tax records would be made available to IRS through the Federal/State Exchange Program." This amounts to nothing less than requiring the various states to make and keep records so that those records can be audited by the IRS. The IRS then in turn audits the people identified from those state records. Such legislation has, as of 1983, been enacted into law by the Commonwealth of Massachusetts.

The justification for this type of interagency and State/Federal involvement is also found in the text of the Plan. It reads like a spy novel. Listen:

> "With the decline of voluntary compliance in a period of budgetary constraints, IRS must find ways to increase "presence" and to selectively apply resources to produce effective results. This initiative should accomplish these purposes. **We are aware that the Board of Governors of the Federal Reserve System, the Federal Deposit Insurance Corporation, the Federal Home Loan Bank Board, the National Credit Union Administration, and the Office of the Comptroller of the Currency conduct examinations as part of their supervision of the institutions that they regulate. A descriptive listing of**

INTRODUCTION 17

> **the investigatory activities performed by these and other federal agencies warrants consideration by Service officials for possible tax implications**.
> (Emphasis added.)

> "Through Interagency Agreements, tax information of a significant nature that is discovered during investigations or examinations by other federal organizations could be furnished to the Service. Since the information would be "significant in nature" (as defined in the Agreement), IRS could selectively pursue those items with potential for substantial compliance impact. Where it is not feasible to pursue an Interagency Agreement, the field could still benefit just by knowing about the existence of other federal activities which might be helpful to IRS investigations."

With the countless agencies of both Federal and State governments now being "audited" by the tax people, the ultimate end suggested by this is that no citizen will escape IRS' watchful eye.

The term "presence" is replete throughout the Plan. In fact, one entire "Statement of Strategic Direction" is dedicated to increasing the "presence" of the IRS in the lives of Americans. It reads:

> "The IRS will seek additional ways to create and maintain a sense of presence and improve our ability to detect sophisticated noncompliance."

They wish to be a totally ubiquitous federal agency. They want you to have — in the back of your mind at all times — in whatever you do and wherever you go — the aching sensation that they are watching you; that they are "present" to observe all your actions and to hear all your conversations. Is there anybody who feels the IRS is not yet sufficiently "present" at this point in their life?

One way in which "presence" will be created and maintained is to "expand our computer-generated contact programs to increase presence." To this end, the IRS will undertake to develop a "taxpayer notification program and a multi-year/ multi-issue" audit program. Rather than wasting time auditing a taxpayer for only one year and one issue, they will undertake to audit for several years and several issues in one swoop. The Plan calls for the immediate implementation of the program. Now, citizens can expect no audit to be a mere perfunctory review of a few receipts and cancelled checks. They can expect that each will be a thorough attic to basement seek-out and examine mission.

Still another method of increasing IRS "presence" and the effectiveness of their audits is to develop a "three-year taxpayer profile" or dossier "which consists of items not found on the tax return." This will be used to supplement the computer processes used "in the selection of returns" for audit. In other words, IRS is building a file on each taxpayer which will contain information not required to be reported on your tax return.

A transcript of the information contained in this dossier would be available to the IRS agent handling your audit. The IRS believes that such a dossier on each individual would "be of special value in uncovering potential unreported income and possible fraud."

What kind of information will the IRS place in their "taxpayer profile"? And why do they need it if it is not required on a tax return?

A reading of the Plan and all the cloak-and-dagger it calls for has led me to one inescapable conclusion: the question of an IRS audit of a given citizen is leaving the realm of possibility and has entered the realm of probability. Are you prepared to deal with the fact that you will be audited? The IRS has explicitly told us it is just a matter of time.

If the IRS is just now coming into its own in the use of technology and the creation of "presence," they have long been astute in the use — or rather misuse — of words to create confusion and misunderstanding. For years they have exploited complex legalese and taxese in communications with the general public knowing full well that the public does not understand such language. One need only peruse the instructions for preparing a 1040 tax return to find validity in this remark.

Ignorance helps to increase the level of public anxiety in their dealings with the IRS and in the assertion of individual rights. Obviously one will not call the IRS to account if he cannot be sure that they have done anything wrong. Similarly, one will not assert one's rights if he is unclear as to what those rights are.

This kind of artificial ignorance was scorned by English lawyer and philosopher John Locke nearly 300 years ago in his diatribe entitled *Of the Abuse of Words*.[10]

In his essay, Locke declared that the use of "learned gibberish" by leaders in society to "perpetually entangle" the masses amounted to "plain cheat and abuse" and could be "imputed to nothing but great folly or greater dishonesty." Locke wisely observed that the only way to "gain admittance or give defense to strange and absurd doctrines is to guard them round about with legions of obscure, doubtful, and undefined words."

Some IRS uses of what Locke called "the art of keeping even inquisitive men from true knowledge" come to mind. The first is "voluntary compliance," a phrase regularly used by the IRS and the only single phrase which appears in the Plan as many times as does the word "presence."

Part of the mission statement is to "encourage and achieve the highest degree of voluntary compliance with the tax laws." If one is free to "volunteer," why must he also "comply"? If he is indeed required and expected to "comply," then the apparent option created by the word "voluntary" is non-existent.

Consider the phrase "withholding allowance," a computation placed upon a Form W-4, Employee's Withholding Allowance Certificate, a form with which every employee is quite familiar. The term "allowance" is universally understood to mean that which is given, as in money, resources, time, etc. On the other hand, the term "withholding" connotes something which is taken away. When used in the same breath, the phrase seems to suggest that IRS is taking away what they have just given.

This phrase "withholding allowance" is probably responsible for more confusion and misunderstanding in the working community than any other the IRS has come up with. These are but two examples of an endless stream of verbiage which, as opined by Locke, has "brought confusion, disorder, and uncertainty into the affairs of mankind; and, if not destroyed, (has) rendered useless those two great rules, religion and justice." The result is that Americans, in pursuit of paying their fair share, have become hopelessly lost in the underbrush of ambiguity.

---
[10] See Locke's **An Essay Concerning Human Understanding**, Vol. II, Book III.

If the Plan has convinced me of anything, it is that this contrived ignorance will continue as a stepping stone on the path to "presence." Contemporaneously with that will be the increased investigative activities which have been only skeletally sketched in this work. The conclusion we must draw from this is that it is now time to crumble the fortress of ignorance erected by the IRS. We must replace it with knowledge and understanding, for only through these institutions can any agency of government, or indeed any government, be held within its lawful boundaries.

Disregard the impulse to say "It won't happen to me. I won't be audited." The odds of its happening to you increase with each passing day as the machinery called for in the Plan is put into place. And I know that the ramifications of an audit or other contact by the IRS can be devastating when heaped upon an ignorant or unsuspecting person.

I have dealt with countless persons who, until that fateful day, walked through their personal or business lives completely oblivious to the dangers lurking in the envelop marked with the return address "Internal Revenue Service." I have looked into the eyes of the person whose life has been plagued with the kind "presence" spoken of in the Plan. I have seen people who, while just yesterday were concerned only with the affairs of their day-to-day lives, are now threatened with deprivation of their very sustenance.

The face of these people is invariably the same. It is painted with the colors of desperation, fear, rage — and always — wonder. It is the kind of a look you would expect to see on a child lost in a huge department store wondering whether the person taking his hand will lead him to his mother or simply represents the next chapter in a bizarre tale of terror and confusion.

So too the questions are often the same. Where do we go from here? What will we do now? How will we live? And lastly — why?

That the IRS has been able to do these things — to create a state of terror in America — is a tribute to the complacency and ignorance of the American people. The solution to the problem, therefore, is and only can be to cure first the complacency and then the ignorance. It is that notion which has given birth to this discourse.

INTRODUCTION 21

You have taken the first, most crucial step to ending the fear which grips the American people about the throat like a schoolyard bully. You have enlisted in basic training in the war of knowledge. The solution indeed is knowledge, for the acquistion of knowledge dispels fear. And with the eradication of fear confidence freely flows. And confidence leads to action, through which positive social change is effected.

REFLECTIONS

We have seen that the IRS, by its own admission, (i.e. the "Strategic" Plan) views its role as that of an army waging war. It is equally evident that the body against whom the war is directed are the American taxpayers. Our concern here is the fashion in which this war will be carried out, and, of course, the minimizing of its casualties. You have seen the ways in which the IRS has and will continue to beef up its war machine, and the ways in which this machine will be directed, in no small way, against you.

After reading the preceding pages, you may have come away with notions questioning the relevance of this work. You may be inclined to think "so what if the IRS expands its computer power? They should be able to catch tax cheats." Or you may conjecture that "since it's their job to collect taxes, they should do so in a way which imposes the least possible cost upon the taxpayer."

Granted — provided that in the process, the very reason and purpose for collecting taxes is not destroyed. Former Supreme Court Justice Oliver Wendell Holmes once noted that taxes are what we pay for "civilized society.[11]
But as Americans, our image of civilization is somewhat more complex than that embraced by, say, an African Bushman. To him, civilization may be nothing more than a dirt road and grass hut with a near-by well. On the other hand, we have come to recognize civilization as not only encompassing all the modern conveniences, but also embodying, in at least as great a way, law and order.

If the cities of our nation were totally without law — were reduced to a sort of jungle barbarism — we would not hold that those cities were "civilized" places to live. The concept

---

[11] Compania General de Tabacos de Filipinas v. Collector of Internal Revenue, 275 U.S. 87 (1927).

that every person has the right to life, liberty and the pursuit of happiness, free of interference from outside forces, is embedded deeply into our heritage. This principle undergirds the American concept of civilization.

So too is the proposition that government was instituted to protect its citizenry. Governments, like people, are subject to a higher law, and only when these laws are observed do we have a truly just government. Thus, while the government does have an obligation to collect money to fund its legitmate functions, when collection is carried out in a mode which violates the law, the government itself has destroyed the very purpose for which the money is to be spent.

We have seen that the IRS has designs to create and maintain a sense of "presence" in the lives of all Americans. We have seen that they have designs to develop a "taxpayer profile" which will include information they don't need for tax purposes. We have seen that they wish to audit certain businesses even though they aren't suspected of owing taxes. Do these actions violate the higher law we all recognize? If our every day-to-day act is subject to constant close scrutiny by the IRS, has the very purpose for which taxes are collected been destroyed in the process? If each person's sovereign existence and peaceful enjoyment of life is made entirely dependent upon his economic worth to the U.S. government, has not the reason for having government in the first place been betrayed?

What is equally clear is that they do not intend to make the kind of changes the Plan envisions in one sweep. Gradual development and implementation of the various programs is called for. Permit me to speculate as to why. Six centuries years before the birth of Christ, a Chinese general named Sun-tzu discussed the art of war in a book by the same title. He said the first, most basic principle of war was to eliminate the enemy's capacity to resist before the out-break of perceptible hostilities. In that way, when the attack comes, the invading army would be met with the least possible resistance. If the enemy is convinced that he cannot win the fight, he will not offer any fight. By modern standards, we refer to this technique as "desensitization through propaganda."

The IRS is using the very same technique to desensitize the average American to the thought of an audit or intensive investigation of his affairs. Each time a particular group of people is attacked by the IRS, and those attacks are published in the national news, Americans become less and less sensitive to IRS attacks. The whole idea becomes more and more acceptable.

Of course, up until now, they have attacked those who "need to be attacked — who don't pay their fair share." We hear of organized crime coming under attack. Who cares about organized crime? They deserve what they get. We hear about tax shelters coming under attack. So what? If anybody makes enough money to afford a tax shelter, they should pay taxes, and plenty of them. We hear about corporations coming under attack. It's about time! We've all known for years that corporations don't pay any taxes.

But with each attack, the IRS comes closer and closer to the average American who doesn't evade taxes, and who doesn't violate the law, and who doesn't have enough money to be able to afford high priced attorneys and accountants to find loopholes in the system. Why has the IRS turned their guns in that direction? The answer is suggested in the context of the plan — to collect more taxes with less expense.

The Big Three — organized crime, corporations and tax shelter investors — can afford to hire the best legal and accounting talent money can buy. With that talent, they can string out the legal process and make it extremly expensive for the IRS to collect. But the average American is, by comparative standards, defenseless. He can't tie up the collection machine because he doesn't understand the labyrinthine legal processes necessary to do so, and he can't afford to buy the knowledge. What's more, he's been rendered immobilized through desensitization. He has been told for so long that "we all have to pay our fair share," he doesn't even stop to wonder what his fair share is. He just pays the bill, whether or not he legally owes it.

If the pattern continues, the IRS will have come full circle, from collecting taxes in order to preserve freedom, to destroying freedom through the collection of taxes.

If we allow ourselves to become desensitized by saying, each time we hear of an IRS attack, "well, they deserve it anyway," we allow the snowball to gain speed and size and weight. Sooner or later it may well crash into our own house.

Just as important as understanding the nature of the IRS' self-styled war is understanding the message of this disquisition. I do not expect you to become a crusader in a Holy War against the IRS. Quite the contrary. If there is anything this country does not need is one more movement, some wild-eyed leaders of which fancy themselves as the only competent managers of governmental affairs.

I submit that you owe it to yourself and your family to take the necessary steps to protect yourself from what very well may be an attack on your property. This is not to say that the lawful amount of taxes legally due and owing should not be paid. They of course should be. But, as Justice Felix Frankfurter once said, "nobody owes any public duty to pay more tax than the law demands: taxes are enforced exactions, not voluntary contributions."[12]

And if, for some reason, either knowingly or unknowingly, the IRS demands money from you which you do not legally owe, don't you think your duty to your family is to prevent their taking it? Is it unreasonable to suggest that you have a right to protect what is lawfully yours?

The IRS itself believes that it's at war, and you are the subject of all its attention. Reading this book will show you how to best protect yourself and your property.

> "If I have set it down it is because that which is clearly known hath less terror than that which is but hinted at and guessed."
>
> Sir Arthur Conan Doyle
> **The Hound of the Baskervilles**

---

[12]*Atlantic Coast Line v. Phillips*, 332 U.S. 168 (1947).

CHRONOLOGICAL LIST OF QUESTIONS ANSWERED

QUESTION 1
If I have nothing to hide, why must I be concerned about an audit?

QUESTION 2
Should I be afraid of the IRS?

QUESTION 3
What is an audit?

QUESTION 4
Who conducts audits?

QUESTION 5
Will an audit always involve a trip to the IRS Office?

QUESTION 6
If I don't file a tax return, how can I be audited?

QUESTION 7
How is my return selected for an audit?

QUESTION 8
During an audit, what will the IRS look for?

QUESTION 9
What's the first thing I should do if notified of an audit?

QUESTION 10
What should I bring to an audit?

QUESTION 11
Must I appear at the time and place specified in the IRS' letter?

QUESTION 12
Should my letters be sent in any special way?

QUESTION 13
Do I have the right to tape record the audit?

26 LIST OF QUESTIONS

QUESTION 14
Do I have the right to witnesses at the audit?

QUESTION 15
Must my tax counsel prepare Form 2848D?

QUESTION 16
What if I refuse to produce certain records at my audit?

QUESTION 17
Should I ever refuse to produce my records?

QUESTION 18
Can I be punished for refusing to produce my records?

QUESTION 19
What can the IRS do to force me to produce my records?

QUESTION 20
What should I do if the IRS serves a summons upon me?

QUESTION 21
What should I do if the IRS begins a summons enforcement proceeding against me?

QUESTION 22
Is a summons enforcement proceeding a criminal case?

QUESTION 23
If I refuse to produce my records, will they always issue a summons?

QUESTION 24
If I'm summoned to bring in my books, can I get witness fees?

QUESTION 25
If the IRS can't get records from me, can they go elsewhere to get them?

QUESTION 26
What must the IRS do to gain access to my bank records?

LIST OF QUESTIONS 27

QUESTION 27
If they can get my records anyway, why shouldn't I just turn them over at the audit?

QUESTION 28
What if I or my counsel cannot get along with the revenue agent?

QUESTION 29
What kind of records do I need to prove my deductions?

QUESTION 30
What if I don't have records?

QUESTION 31
How long should I keep my records?

QUESTION 32
How many times can I be audited for a single year?

QUESTION 33
When is a case considered closed?

QUESTION 34
What will happen when the audit is complete?

QUESTION 35
Must I always pay the amount they say I owe?

QUESTION 36
How do I make an appeal to the Appeals Office?

QUESTION 37
Can IRS send me a bill without giving me an opportunity to appeal?

QUESTION 38
Can I negotiate a settlement with the examiner?

QUESTION 39
What penalties can be added to a tax bill?

QUESTION 40
When will interest be included in a tax bill?

QUESTION 41
Am I responsible for mistakes made by my return perparer?

28 LIST OF QUESTIONS

QUESTION 42
If you were to diagram the various levels of the IRS that we've discussed so far, what would it look like?

QUESTION 43
Why must I be concerned about appeals?

QUESTION 44
When can an appeal be taken?

QUESTION 45
Can I always appeal my case?

QUESTION 46
Does the tax have to be paid before I can Appeal?

QUESTION 47
Must I take my case to the Appeals Office before going to court?

QUESTION 48
Do I have a choice of where to appeal my case?

QUESTION 49
What's the difference between the administrative and judicial appeal routes?

QUESTION 50
Which court is more desirable, the Tax Court or the District Court?

QUESTION 51
Where is my administrative appeal filed?

QUESTION 52
What must I do to take a judicial appeal?

QUESTION 53
How is a claim for refund filed?

QUESTION 54
When can I file my suit for refund?

QUESTION 55
Will I get a hearing in my administrative appeal?

QUESTION 56
What procedures are followed at an appeals conference?

LIST OF QUESTIONS 29

QUESTION 57
Can I have counsel with me at the conference?

QUESTION 58
Can I have witnesses present at the conference?

QUESTION 59
How will I be expected to present my case?

QUESTION 60
What is the difference between law and fact?

QUESTION 61
How are the facts best presented?

QUESTION 62
How is the law best presented?

QUESTION 63
Will I receive only one Appeals conference?

QUESTION 64
What basis is used by Appeals Officers to make decisions?

QUESTION 65
Can I negotiate with the Appeals Officer?

QUESTION 66
How are cases settled at the Appeals level?

QUESTION 67
What will happen if we cannot reach an agreement?

QUESTION 68
How long will it take the notice of deficiency to issue?

QUESTION 69
Can I appeal the notice of deficiency?

QUESTION 70
Can I change from the Tax Court to the District Court, or vise-versa?

QUESTION 71
Who will represent the IRS in court?

QUESTION 72
What kind of trial can I expect?

30 LIST OF QUESTIONS

QUESTION 73
How long will it take the court to decide my case?

QUESTION 74
Can I appeal the decision of the court?

QUESTION 75
What exactly is a Small Tax Case?

QUESTION 76
When do I appeal the decision of the court?

QUESTION 77
If you were to diagram the various courts that we've just discussed, what would it look like?

QUESTION 78
Why should I be concerned about "enforced collection?" I pay my taxes.

QUESTION 79
Who collects money for the IRS?

QUESTION 80
When will I be contacted by Collection?

QUESTION 81
Will I always be audited before I am sent a bill?

QUESTION 82
What if I get a bill for taxes I don't think I owe?

QUESTION 83
Must I use any special language when objecting to an improper bill?

QUESTION 84
Will they try to collect even after my letter of protest?

QUESTION 85
What can I do if they try to collect money which I don't owe?

QUESTION 86
Are there any circumstances in which a tax may be assessed without regard to the deficiency procedures?

QUESTION 87
Are there limitations which apply to jeopardy assessments?

LIST OF QUESTIONS 31

QUESTION 88
Are jeopardy assessments appealable?

QUESTION 89
Can I sue the IRS?

QUESTION 90
What can the IRS do to "enforce collection" of taxes?

QUESTION 91
How much of my paycheck can be seized?

QUESTION 92
Can my homestead be seized?

QUESTION 93
If I own property jointly with my spouse, can it still be seized?

QUESTION 94
If my spouse signed a joint return but didn't have income, can she be made to pay the tax?

QUESTION 95
Can I avoid seizure of my property by just giving it away?

QUESTION 96
What property is exempt from seizure?

QUESTION 97
Can my pension or Social Security payments be levied?

QUESTION 98
How long does the IRS have to collect a tax?

QUESTION 99
How long does a tax lien last?

QUESTION 100
Are there any limitations on the manner in which the IRS may execute its levy?

QUESTION 101
Can I be made to pay the tax debts of a corporation?

QUESTION 102
How do I contest the 100 percent penalty?

QUESTION 103
If my property is held in trust, can it be seized?

LIST OF QUESTIONS

QUESTION 104
What rules must be followed when the IRS sells seized property?

QUESTION 105
Can I redeem seized property?

QUESTION 106
If I owe taxes, will I always have to deal with Automated Collection?

QUESTION 107
How should I pay taxes once Collection has the case?

QUESTION 108
After taxes are paid, will the liens be lifted?

QUESTION 109
Can I enter into a payment agreement with the IRS?

QUESTION 110
Can I negotiate the tax with Collection?

QUESTION 111
How do I make an offer in compromise?

QUESTION 112
If I don't "evade" my taxes, why do I have to worry about a criminal prosecution?

QUESTION 113
What are the different types of tax offenses?

QUESTION 114
What does the term "willfullness" mean?

QUESTION 115
What is the difference between tax "evasion" and tax "avoidance"?

QUESTION 116
Is tax avoidance legal?

QUESTION 117
Is there a statute of limitations on tax offenses?

QUESTION 118
What does the typical criminal investigation involve?

LIST OF QUESTIONS

QUESTION 119
What in particular are Special Agents looking for?

QUESTION 120
If I'm under criminal investigation, why can't I just pay the tax they think I owe?

QUESTION 121
Which aspects of a tax case are decided first, the civil or criminal?

QUESTION 122
If I am prosecuted for a tax offense, am I still liable for civil penalties?

QUESTION 123
What basis is used to determine who will be prosecuted?

QUESTION 124
How is the typical criminal investigation begun?

QUESTION 125
When will I learn that I'm under criminal investigation?

QUESTION 126
Should I answer any questions asked by the special agent?

QUESTION 127
If I choose not to answer any of his questions, what should I tell him?

QUESTION 128
When can I have my counsel present with me?

QUESTION 129
How long does a criminal investigation take?

QUESTION 130
What will happen when the special agent has completed his investigation?

QUESTION 131
What role does District Counsel play?

QUESTION 132
Will I be notified if the Special Agent has referred my case to District Counsel?

34 LIST OF QUESTIONS

QUESTION 133
Should I meet with District Counsel if I am invited to confer with them?

QUESTION 134
What will District Counsel do with the case after they've evaluated it?

QUESTION 135
Will I be notified if District Counsel makes a formal recommendation for prosecution in my case?

QUESTION 136
Can the Justice Department reject the recommendation for prosecution?

QUESTION 137
Will I be notified if Justice approves the recommendation?

QUESTION 138
What is a grand jury?

QUESTION 139
Do I have the right to appear before the grand jury?

QUESTION 140
Can my grand jury testimony be used against me in my trial?

QUESTION 141
What will happen if the grand jury decides to indict me?

QUESTION 142
How long before I am brought to trial?

QUESTION 143
What should I do if I am charged with a crime?

QUESTION 144
If you were to diagram the criminal investigatory process, what would it look like?

QUESTION 145
The IRS has never before posed any problem in my dealings with third parties. Why should I be concerned all of a sudden?

QUESTION 146
What do I report to my Employer on Form W-4?

LIST OF QUESTIONS   35

QUESTION 147
If I expect to pay no taxes during the current year, must I submit to withholding?

QUESTION 148
Will the IRS ever see my W-4 Form?

QUESTION 149
Must I file a Form W-4?

QUESTION 150
Can I change my Form W-4 after it has been filed?

QUESTION 151
Must independent contractors file Form W-4?

QUESTION 152
What's the difference between an independent contractor and an employee?

QUESTION 153
Why has my bank recently demanded my Social Security number?

QUESTION 154
What kind of payments are subject to the new withholding law?

QUESTION 155
Must I give my Social Security number to anyone who asks for it?

QUESTION 156
Does the IRS require an SSN for tax filings?

QUESTION 157
If I don't have the money to pay my taxes, should I file the return without the money?

QUESTION 158
Can I get an extension of time to pay the tax?

QUESTION 159
Is my tax return and its information confidential?

QUESTION 160
Who is the IRS?

36 LIST OF QUESTIONS

QUESTION 161
When did the IRS come into existence?

QUESTION 162
How is the IRS organized?

QUESTION 163
What is "The Law"?

PREVIEW TO THIS WORK

The one branch of IRS with which a citizen is most likely to come into direct contact is the Compliance Branch. This branch staffs IRS personnel whose duty it is to see that the internal revenue laws, as they read them, are complied with. Their interests therefore fall into the general areas of collecting taxes, auditing tax returns and investigating possible criminal violations of the tax code. Four divisions of the Compliance branch will be examined in this work, as each is responsible for direct taxpayer contact. They are:

1. Examination. This division is the one which conducts all audits of income tax returns, both of individuals and other entities, such as corporations. Persons working in this division are called Revenue Agents.

2. Appeals. This division handles appeals of disputed decisions of revenue agents made in connection with an audit. For example, if after an audit the revenue agent determines that an additional sum of money is due, his decision may be appealed. The appeal is heard by an Appeals Officer.

3. Collection. This division is made up of Revenue Officers whose duty it is to collect unpaid federal taxes. Think of this division as the federal collection agency. Revenue Officers are the IRS employees who make seizures of businesses, such property as bank accounts and automobiles, and levy paychecks, to settle unpaid tax depts.

4. Criminal Investigation. This division handles the cloak-and-dagger type investigations of taxpayers suspected of "tax fraud." Employees here are called Special Agents, and they gather the evidence which is ultimately used in the prosecution of citizens for any of the several criminal violations enumerated in the tax code.

Each of the next four chapters will look at one of the divisions mentioned above. The questions and answers are designed to give you, the reader, a comprehensive overview of the internal workings of the IRS, and more then a casual look at your rights and how they may be used to protect yourself and your property.

The fifth chapter will discuss general, miscellaneous questions about the IRS, and Chapter Six will answer the Ultimate Question, What is the **Law?**

Chapter One
THE KNOCK ON THE DOOR
Questions Relating to Audit

Background to this Chapter—

Before a "tax return" can be audited, a return of course must be filed. Tax returns are filed by individuals, corporations, trusts, partnerships, and estates. Any return filed with the IRS is subject to audit by them. In recent years, the IRS has opted to use the term "examination" rather than "audit" to refer to the act of "determining the correctness" of a return. Whichever term you prefer to use is academic; the process is the same.

Once a return is received at the IRS office, it is reviewed for completeness. Reviewing personnel will determine whether it has been signed, whether a check for taxes is included if taxes are due, and whether all of the necessary schedules are attached and complete. They will also check for obvious mathematical errors.

Once this is done, the information on the return is fed into the master computer and a document called a Certificate of Assessments and Payments, Form 4340, is prepared and maintained in the computer file. Form 4340 shows the date the return was filed, the amount of income claimed on the return, the amount of tax withheld during the course of the year, the amount of the tax liability, and the amount of refund or balance due.

While a printout of this form can and routinely is made for several reasons, the information is primarily compiled for computer purposes to facilitate records searches. These searches enable the IRS to discover whether a person has failed to make a required tax return in a particular year.

The computer file is created and "accessed" by your Social Security number, or as the IRS refers to it, your Taxpayer Identification number. Without this number, it is impossible for the IRS to create, access or maintain any records in their computer system. One Revenue Officer testified in a court hearing in Minneapolis, Minnesota, that the IRS cannot begin to even search their records without an SS number. The Social Security number, therefore, is the linchpin upon which the entire federal tax apparatus swings.

THE KNOCK ON THE DOOR 39

Once the information is filed in the computer, the return is given a document locator number so that it can be found for future reference if need be. The tax is then assessed, or recorded as due and owing. If it is paid in full, either with a check or through wage withholding, the assessment is marked paid. Where appropriate, a refund check is generated by the computer. If the tax is not paid for some reason, payment demand notices will be mailed. If necessary, the matter will be placed into the hands of the Collection Division for collection.

From this point, returns are selected for audit. In addition, when the computer discovers a failure to file by persons or organizations apparently "required" to file, a return will be demanded of them. Exactly how returns are selected for audit will be discussed later.

QUESTION 1
If I have nothing to hide, why must I be concerned about an audit?

Everybody has heard, and maybe asked, if you have nothing to hide, why should you be afraid of an audit? If I have all my records to support the claims and deductions taken on the return, what can the IRS possibly do about it? There is some logic in these statements, and under ordinary circumstances this line of thinking would be difficult to refute.

However, we are not now faced with ordinary circumstances. As we have seen from the Introduction, the IRS has declared war on the average American. The reason: It is determined to collect more taxes with less effort and cost. This seems like a lofty goal worthy of the support of the American taxpayer, but in the final analysis the only one who cannot afford to protect himself against unlawful IRS action is the average American himself.

He cannot afford high-priced lawyers and accountants to prove to the IRS that his return is correct and proper and that he doesn't owe additional taxes. He cannot afford the cost of litigation if the IRS takes a contrary position with respect to his return. In short, he is at the mercy of the IRS.

The IRS, better than anybody, knows this and intends to capitalize on this fact. The Plan tells us that audit and collection activity will be greatly increased. It tells us that the IRS will broaden its search and tighten its grip on middle

America because it cannot efficiently collect taxes from the Big Three.[1]

As a result, no longer can we expect to receive a "clean bill of health" from the IRS after an audit is complete, whether or not we have records. We can expect our deductions and other claims to be disallowed. We can expect to be put to the test of litigating those claims and deductions. We can expect that the IRS will make us jump through all the necessary hoops to prove our entitlement to any claim made.

So even though you may "have nothing to hide" before the audit, you very well may have "something to prove" when the audit is finished. If you know how to do it, you have nothing to fear. If you don't, you'd better learn or prepare to hire legal talent to do it for you. Records or no records, you can expect the IRS to point its collection guns in your direction.

QUESTION 2
Should I be afraid of the IRS?

Several years ago, Parade Magazine ran a feature article on the IRS entitled *Why you should FEAR the IRS*. The article was full of horror stories about how the IRS seizes property, puts people out of their homes and businesses and in general, almost indiscriminately destroys lives. CBS' *60 Minutes* did a similar expose', as did former Congressman George Hansen, in a book entitled **To Harass Our People**. The common thread running through the fabric of each of these well-documented accounts is the awesome power which agents of the IRS have, and the fact that they use it — a lot.

Continued presentation of these newsworthy and well-done accounts of IRS abuses has had a side-effect probably not intended by their creators. People see and hear examples of the incredible power the IRS has, and rather than stand up for their rights when confronted with such power, they roll over to whatever demands are made upon them, whether or not lawful. The fear generated by the kind of reporting mentioned above has a tendency to immobilize people. After all, who wants to be next month's horror story?

The IRS itself orchestrates terror publicity regularly. In the spring of every year, year after year, newspaper headlines all

---

[1] See the Introduction.

over the country herald accounts of the unfortunates who have been criminally charged with "tax evasion." The stories always appear just before the April 15th filing deadline. Have you ever asked yourself why people are seemingly indicted for tax crimes only in the spring of the year, just before April 15th?

The Plan calls upon the IRS to make its "presence" felt in the lives of all Americans. The establishment and maintenance of "presence" is one more tact in the overall strategy of immobilizing the populace through fear. The more terrorized you are of the IRS, the more abuses the IRS will be able to get away with.

I say to **heck** with the fear. If you know what your rights are and how to make them stick, you do not have to be emasculated by fear. If you aren't afraid of the IRS, then you can't be taken advantage of by them.

The fact of the matter is, with the recent trend in drunk-driving laws the way it is, you have far more to fear by getting a DWI citation then you have cause for concern over the IRS. If you know their limits and force them to stay within those limits, you have nothing to fear no matter how much bureaucratic saber-rattling goes on.

QUESTION 3
What is an audit?

While we principally think of an audit as sitting down with a tax examiner who carefully looks at all our books and records, tax audits can and usually do take many forms. The act of carefully scrutinizing receipts and cancelled checks is only one form of audit.

The typical tax audit consists of an examination of a filed tax return for purposes of "determining its correctness." That is, your return is examined to determine whether you can in fact prove that you are entitled to the various deductions, exemptions, and credits you may have claimed on the return. In this kind of audit, you'll be asked to produce the books and records of account maintained by you in order to justify the various expenses claimed.

However, audits are not limited to just an examination of expenses, and can involve the review of records other than your own. It is possible that an audit may consist of nothing more than an administrative review of the tax return itself, without ever looking at your supporting documentation.

In addition, you may be audited to determine the extent of — not expenses claimed — but rather, income shown on your return. In this context, an audit will involve your having to produce all records of bank deposits, including deposit slips and bank statements. You would also be required to demonstrate the extent of your wages, or if self-employed, your gross receipts. You would also have to disclose records of purchases and sales, such as transactions involving stocks, bonds, commodities, real estate, or other personal property, such as cars, boats, etc. They can also be expected to look at checking account interest, Christmas bonuses, employee benefits, and other items of income which may not be reported on tax returns, but are easily traced.

This kind of tax audit — the income audit — is increasing in frequency, particularly in light of the Plan. The IRS is convinced that middle America is, as a group, cheating on their tax returns, and that such cheating is not limited to just claiming improper deductions. IRS is determined to track down "unreported income."

They believe that the so-called underground economy is responsible for evading hundreds of millions of dollars in taxes every year, and they have set a plan in motion to stop it. You are the target. Consequently, you can expect future audits to focus at least as much attention, if not more, on the income side of the scale as past audits have focused on the expense side.

Consistent with this attitude, you can expect the IRS to make direct contact with your bank, your employer and others with whom you do business. You can expect that more and more the IRS will canvass third party sources of information looking for those elusive underground tax evaders. In the Introduction, we have analyzed the various sources which the IRS will pursue in an effort to catch these "tax cheats." The only problem is that everybody is perceived as a tax cheat. Concomitantly, everybody will be subject to the financial dragnet about to be dropped.

Another increasingly more common form of audit is the administrative review of your tax return. In this kind of audit, the IRS looks at your return without informing you that they are doing so. Under the auspices of determining whether your arithmatic is correct, they look at all the entries on the return. When finished, a bill is mailed. The bill says that a mathematical error was discovered on the return and after correction additional taxes are due. The bills, called "mathematical recomputations," are usually relatively small — anywhere from $200 to $1,500.

The bill demands payment of the additional tax, providing no explanation other than that "an error was discovered" on your tax return. It is usually impossible to get any clarification as to what the error was and how it effected your tax liability. IRS simply demands payment or else.

The Plan has specifically called for the increase in "computer generated contacts" presumably because of the relatively low cost of conducting this kind of audit. With nothing more than a postage stamp, the IRS can collect from an unsuspecting citizen as much as $1,500 or more. All it takes is the audacity to send the bill.

QUESTION 4
Who Conducts Audits?

Audits are conducted by the Examination Division. Personnel which staff this division are called Revenue Agents. Revenue Agents will sit with you during your audit and will actually look at your return and its supporting documentation.

QUESTION 5
Will an audit always involve a trip to the IRS Office?

Ordinarily, you will have to go to the IRS office for the audit. However, in the cases of businesses and corporations, it is not unusual for the IRS to come to the office of the business they intend to audit.

Many people are concerned about going to the IRS Office for an audit. The thought of meeting the enemy on his own turf unsettles them. These feelings are valid. If possible, you may suggest to the agent that the audit may take place in your counsel's office, or your own office if you prefer. Whether they agree to this kind of review will be dependent upon the agent involved, but it can't hurt to ask.

QUESTION 6
If I don't file a tax return, how can I be audited?

In the sense of a conventional audit, you can't be, as a conventional audit consists of the review of a return to

44   THE KNOCK ON THE DOOR

determine its correctness. This is not to say, however, that one can't be contacted for an explanation as to why no return was filed.

In addition to receiving tax returns, IRS Regional Service Centers are also responsible for receiving and assimilating hundreds of millions of information returns each year. An information return is a document filed with the IRS which reports only information, and which does not directly involve the payment of any tax.

The best example of an information return is a Form W-2, Wage and Tax Statement. All employees receive such a form from their employer at the end of the year, usually by January 31st of the following year. The W-2 shows how much money you were paid in wages, how much was withheld for federal and state tax purposes, and what was taken out for Social Security. Other wage deductions, such as pension contributions, are also shown.

Service Center computers are programmed to cross-check information returns with tax returns to determine whether persons required to file a 1040 have in fact filed one. The sheer volume of information returns and tax returns the IRS is required to process each year makes it impossible to achieve 100% accuracy in this process. However, the IRS claims that their ability to cross-check hovers around the 75% mark. This means that for every four persons represented by information returns, the IRS will be able to identify three of them by their tax return.

As we have learned from the Plan, the IRS intends to install optical scanning equipment in an effort to beef up the "safety net" that information returns provide. I have speculated that when the system is fully operational, everthing you earn, buy and sell will be reported to the IRS on an information return, filed and recorded by your Social Security, or Taxpayer Identification number.

Presently, if a return is not filed and the IRS has information returns which show the receipt of what they consider income, a Form 8176 will be sent to the individual. That form inquires as to why a return was not filed when IRS records show that one should have been. If the IRS receives no response to this letter, or the response they do receive is not satisfactory, further follow up will eventually lead to a situation where a revenue agent is assigned to the case with instructions to prepare a return for the citizen, either with or without his cooperation.[2] After that, the individual is sent what amounts to a bill for the tax shown in the return so prepared.

QUESTION 7
How is my return selected for audit?

There are essentially two kinds of tax audits currently in existence. The manner in which your return is selected is dependent upon which type of audit you are about to undergo. The first and most common method of selecting a return for audit is through the Discriminant Function (DIF) system. Under this system, a complex computer program classifies tax returns according to their potential for change. The higher the potential for change, the greater the possibility that return will be selected for audit.

The DIF system operates using two classes of tax returns, nonbusiness returns and business returns. Once categorized in either of those classes, the return is assigned a formula based upon the amount of total income shown on the return. Business returns are assigned formulas on the basis of gross receipts.

Then, using the formula applicable to the amount of income shown on the return, complicated computations are performed on each line of the return, evaluating the exemptions claimed, deductions, filing status, etc. There are literally hundreds of variables considered by the computer. If, after the computations are performed, a particular item on the return is identified as a high potential area, that return will be selected for audit.

The second way in which returns are selected is under the Taxpayer Compliance Measurement Program (TCMP). TCMP is a research program developed for the purpose of updating the DIF formulas. Under TCMP, a return is selected on a completely random basis using only ending digits of the Social Security number. TCMP audits are done at approximately three-year intervals.

The greater the IRS' ability to compile and assimilate information about individual returns, the greater will be their ability to audit each return. Hence, the beefing-up of the entire IRS computer system. Once the changes are made in the

---
[2] See Code §6020(b).

overall computer system consistent with ideas called for in the Plan, it should be possible for IRS to audit every return filed every year. The Plan has indicated that this is a major IRS goal.

A third, less discussed method of selecting people for audit is based upon their potential for turning up so-called "tax cheats." As we have seen, people and businesses are audited to discover whether their customers are cheating. Also, the intra-governmental cross-checking called for in the Plan seems to indicate that the IRS will more and more rely upon outside leads to generate audits. Their goal to collect more taxes with less effort suggests that they must concentrate on those areas which will produce the most fruitful results. I project intensified audit activity on the basis of hit lists so developed.

QUESTION 8
During an audit, what will the IRS look for?

The answer to this depends upon the way in which the return was selected. If it was selected by the DIF system, the item which the computer identified as susceptible to change will be looked at. For example, if the computer flags your interest deduction as particularly high for your income bracket, the audit will focus on the interest deduction.

If the return is selected as part of the TCMP program or from a list, the entire return will be looked over from beginning to end. Generally, a taxpayer under audit can expect to have his itemized deductions looked at rather carefully by the IRS.

QUESTION 9
What's the first thing I should do if notified of an audit?

We must ask a few questions in order to answer this question. First of all, did you have your return prepared by a professional preparer? If so, contact the preparer immediately. Not for the purpose of hiring the preparer to represent you at the audit, but to put him on notice that you have been called in for an audit and that you may need the information which you provided for the preparation of your return.

Next, look at the notification which you have received from the IRS. It will be one of two basic forms. The first will state that your return was selected for audit and **certain items** on

THE KNOCK ON THE DOOR 47

the return must be verified. The letter may flag your interest and medical expense deductions, for example.

If your notice is in this form, your return was probably selected through the DIF program. During your audit, you will be expected to verify those items. You should therefore proceed to put together the information needed to verify the items singled out. Use Form 1040 and its attachments as a guide. If you claimed $1,400 in interest, as an illustration, gather the records which support $1,400 worth of interest paid during the year in question.

If your notice of audit takes the second form, other steps should be taken. The second form I'm referring to is the simple letter which contains words to the effect that your return has been selected for audit: "please bring **all of your books and records** which show the receipt of income and the payment of deductible expenses for the year in question."

This kind of audit I would refer to as a fishing expedition. The IRS wants to look at everything from income to the last penny's worth of expenses. This kind of audit can be engendered in one of two ways. Either you have been selected as part of the TCMP program, or you are on a hit list for some reason.

Due to the exposure involved in this kind of audit, it is a good idea to limit your involvement to the fullest extent possible. The way to do this is, prior to appearing at the meeting scheduled in the letter, write to the revenue agent and ask him to pin down the specific items on the return which are in question.

Many times, when asked, the revenue agent will look at the return and, using personal judgment, select only those items which appear questionable. You will then bring with you to the audit only those items which have been isolated by the agent. In this way, you can prevent yourself from being subjected to a painstaking review of your personal affairs.

Once you have determined the kind of audit you are probably into, you can take the next step, if you deem it necessary. This would be to consult counsel. If you feel it necessary to employ the services of a tax professional, be sure to have this person retained and fully apprised of the issues prior to the audit. You should have placed in his possession a copy of your return, the letter from the IRS, and copies of the documentation you have to support the items claimed. You will want your counsel present with you at the audit.

QUESTION 10
What should I bring to the Audit?

What you should bring in the way of documentation will chiefly depend upon what items are to be audited. Refer to your letter from the IRS, or to the answer you received from the revenue agent in response to your letter. (See Question 9.) The items designated in these letters will be the documentation you will need.

You should also bring with you a pad of paper, a pencil and, if you deem it necessary, your tax professional. As simple as this seems, most people slink into the audit with nothing but a shoebox full of receipts and cancelled checks. When questions arise which require follow up, they are unprepared to capture the question and make the notes necessary to ensure the proper follow up. More than one person has been denied deductions they were legally entitled to because they didn't follow up properly.

An IRS audit can be a very high-tension situation. Believe it or not, unless you go through them all the time, you won't remember your own name going in, and won't remember the day of the week coming out. Be sure to have pencil and paper to take careful notes.

One more thing, you should have photocopies of your documentation with you when you go in. Invariably, the agent will want to keep your originals to make copies. This is unacceptable. You must always retain your originals for possible future use. The agent is entitled to nothing more than legible copies. You should, however, have your originals with you at the audit.

QUESTION 11
Must I appear at the time and place specified in the IRS' letter?

Although the flavor of the audit notice will suggest that you must appear on that day and at that location, you are not irreversibly committed to this date and place. If there is a date and place which is more convenient for you, a letter to the agent suggesting the alternative is usually sufficient to accomplish the change.

Obviously, the place you set for the audit will have to be a reasonable location. I don't think the IRS will agree to change your audit from Memphis, Tennessee, to Sidney, Australia.

THE KNOCK ON THE DOOR

Nor will they agree to conduct the audit at the local television station.

You are entitled, however, to accommodate yourself to the fullest extent possible. If an IRS office other than the one they've selected would be more convenient, you may insist upon a meeting there. Also, your own office or that of your counsel may be advisable in certain circumstances. Don't be afraid to ask.

QUESTION 12
Should my letters be sent in any special way?

Yes. You must keep in mind that whenever you deal with the IRS at any level, there is always the possibility of litigation. For this reason, whenever you correspond with them, your letters should be sent **via** certified mail, with a return receipt requested. You should also keep a photocopy of your letter for your own file.

When you send certified mail, you receive two separate receipts from the Post Office. The white receipt is for postage paid. The green card bears the signature of the person to whom the letter was addressed. This card is your proof, should the question ever come up, that the addressee in fact received your letter.

The first one you'll get from the postal clerk when you mail the letter. The second you'll get in the mail a few days after your letter was received and signed for by the addressee. When you have both receipts in your hand, staple them to your photocopy of the letter. This will ensure an accurate record of when each letter was sent and received.

QUESTION 13
Do I have a right to tape record the audit?

Yes, but the IRS will never tell you this. In fact, if you simply show up at your audit and produce a tape recorder, the agent will probably panic and terminate the conference. For some reason, unannounced tape recorders have the same effect in an IRS office that a crucifix has at a vampire convention. Why? — I can only guess.

The point is that if you announce ahead of the conference — such as in your letter — that you intend to record it, my experience has been that you will encounter no opposition. You will notice, however, that the agent is also recording the meeting.

QUESTION 14
Do I have a right to witnesses at the audit?

Yes, but again the IRS will not generally tell you this. The rhetoric is that your tax return and related information are privileged material and nobody has the right to see it. While this is true, the citizen has the right to disclose to any person his confidential tax information.[3] So while the agent will explain that your witnesses must be excluded from the conference "for your own benefit," you can explain that the law entitles you to the witness.

In fact, the IRS has issued a form which permits you to give written authorization to any witness you choose. IRS Form 2848D, Authorization and Declaration, can be obtained from the IRS and filled out with the name and address of your witness. Once this form is signed by the citizen and given to the agent, there is no lawful way your witness can be excluded from the meeting.

QUESTION 15
Must my tax counsel prepare Form 2848D?

A person acting as counsel to a citizen in a tax matter will generally not prepare Form 2848D, but rather will prepare Form 2848, Power of Attorney. The difference in the two is that the former merely authorizes the named person to receive confidential tax information. The latter, on the other hand, authorizes the named representative to actually speak in behalf of, and to generally represent the citizen in the controversy.

There are limitations on who can use a 2848, Power of Attorney. These limitations can be broken into a few areas. One must be either a licensed attorney, a certified public accountant, or a person enrolled to practice before the IRS. Enrollment is accomplished by passing a test administered by the Treasury Department.

Under special circumstances, persons not falling into those areas can represent another. For example, an officer or full-time employee of an organization, such as a corporation, may represent that organization. Or, a member of the citizen's immediate family may act as a representative for that person. The rules for representation of others before the IRS are set out in Treasury Department Circular No. 230.

---

[3] See §6103 of the IRS Code.

THE KNOCK ON THE DOOR 51

QUESTION 16
What if I refuse to produce certain records at my audit?

Believe it or not, refusal to comply with IRS requests for records is not as uncommon as one might believe. The little known fact is that the IRS agent himself is powerless to force anybody to produce anything. The only body which has that kind of power is the United States Courts.

There are, however, consequences for failing to produce records. The most common and likely consequence of failing to produce records is that the specific deduction for which the record is sought will be disallowed.

As the IRS and the courts are so fond of saying, "deductions are a matter of legislative grace." That is to say, Congress has been very considerate and giving of itself when it allows you to deduct your interest, medical, charitable contribution and other expenses. If you don't prove that you incurred the expenses, the IRS will not allow the expenses. Thus, disallowance of the claimed item is the most common and immediate consequence of failure to produce records, but there are other considerations.

For example, if the agent is convinced he needs the records, he could serve upon you a summons, Form 2039, demanding that you produce the records. The summons is akin to a subpoena and issues under the authority of §7602 of the IRS Code. This form will state that you are required to produce the stated records at a specified time, date and place. But again, the IRS itself is powerless to force you to produce the records, even with a summons. They must look to the United States Courts for enforcement.

QUESTION 17
Should I ever refuse to produce my records?

The Fifth Amendment to the United States Constitution provides that no person can be compelled to be a witness against himself. In years past, the courts have extended this protection to the production of personal books and records to the IRS in an audit. Thus, at one time, if a person had cause to believe that his books and records could somehow be used against him, he had the right to refuse to produce or give testimony about them.

Recently, the Supreme Court has held that a person **does not** have the right to refuse to produce books and records on ground of the Fifth Amendment. The decision, **United States v. Doe**[4] is revolutionary in light of the literally hundreds of decisions enforcing one's right to do so. However, the Court has continued to hold that one need not give actual testimony about his personal affairs.

As a result of this recent holding, the process of claiming one's Fifth Amendment rights is far more intricate then is Constitutionally called for. If one wishes to assert those rights, according to the Supreme Court, his refusal is now limited to answering the question whether the records exist, since that is a matter of testimony protected by the Fifth Amendment. He may not, however, refuse to produce the records on the ground of the Fifth Amendment if it is established that they do exist.

The hair-splitting amounts to simply this: If you admit that your records exist, then you will be forced to produce them. If you refuse to admit or deny that the records exist, then IRS could not gain access to them, since in order to do so they must first establish with credible testimony that they in fact exist. This of course couldn't be done if you yourself refused to do so.

Whether or not it is advisable for any one person to assert this right depends upon the facts and circumstances of each case. Extreme caution must abound where an assertion of the right is concerned. A careful reading of the **Doe** case should be your first step. You must then weigh the pros and cons of refusing production, paying particular attention to the risk of production you believe exits.

You may also wish to consult counsel knowledgeable on the availability of the right, and the procedures for asserting it. The counsel who says: "It's illegal, you can't do it," is not the one with whom to discuss it. Most tax preparers have no practical knowledge of tax litigation rules. Keep this in mind when dealing with the typical tax preparer. Counsel with experience in the precise area is most desirable.

QUESTION 18
Can I be punished for refusing to produce my records?

If you told the revenue agent that you were refusing to produce certain records demanded, you will most probably be met with a barrage of verbal assaults. The aggression will take

---

[4]104 S.Ct. 1237 (1984).

the form of threats from everything from fine to imprisonment. Under these circumstances, agents will usually point to §7210 of the Code. This section provides penalties of up to a $1,000 fine and one year in prison for failure to obey an IRS summons for records.

It must be noted that failure to deliver records in an audit and failure to obey a summons[5] are two entirely different things. Section 7210 cannot be made to apply where no summons has been issued.

You will know when you've been formally summoned to bring your records to the IRS. The summons document, Form 2039, states at the top in bold, black letters "SUMMONS," and goes on to describe in detail the records you are to bring to the IRS. In an audit, you are before the IRS by virtue of a mere letter requesting your attendance.

Strictly speaking, in the context of an audit, there is nothing the IRS can do to punish you for refusing to produce your records, other than to disallow your deductions.

QUESTION 19
What can the IRS do to force me to produce my records?

There are two ways for the IRS to proceed in the face of such a refusal. First and most likely is that they will simply disallow the deductions claimed on the return. The second course of action is for the agent to issue a summons for your records. The summons issues under §7602 and demands that you produce the records.

The summons requires that you appear at a certain time, date and place, and before a certain IRS agent to produce records and give testimony relative to your receipt of income and payment of expenses for certain years. The summons is an administrative demand for the production of records. It does have teeth.

For example, if you refuse, without good cause, to comply with the summons, the IRS could seek an enforcement order from the local United States District Court. This involves the filing of a civil lawsuit by the United States Attorney on behalf of the IRS. The suit would ask the court to order you to turn your records over to the IRS so that they can complete their examination of your financial affairs.

---

[5] Summonses will be discussed in detail at Questions 19-26.

Keep in mind that the IRS, by themselves, are powerless to force you to do anything. They must apply to the district court for an order forcing you to comply with their wishes. You, of course, have the opportunity to be heard before the court issues any order regarding your records. You have the opportunity to voice any objection you have to providing the records demanded.

If you can successfully persuade a judge that the IRS ought not to have access to the demanded records, the court will not order them released. On the other hand, if you cannot successfully accomplish this, you will be ordered to deliver the records forthwith. Having been ordered to release your records, you have the obligation to comply with the court's order. If you fail to do so, you could be held in contempt of court and punished. Such punishment could include fine and imprisonment for each day that your failure to obey the order continues.

In past experience, the only argument consistently successful in preventing IRS access to personal records has been the Fifth Amendment objection. However, we must now read the Fifth Amendment in the light — jaundiced though it is — cast upon it by the Supreme Court's decision in the **Doe** case.

For a Fifth Amendment argument to be successful, one cannot admit that any records exist. Once such an admission is made, the court will rule that the Fifth Amendment does not attach to the records themselves, and would order them turned over. But one could refuse to give **testimony** — which is protected by the Fifth Amendment — as to the existence of the books and records, in which case the IRS must **prove** they exist. If it cannot be proved that the records exist and are in your possession, they cannot legally gain access to them.

QUESTION 20
What should I do if the IRS serves a summons upon me?

The Supreme Court, in **Reisman v. Caplin**,[6] held that upon service of a summons, the citizen must appear at the time and place set out in the summons, and may then object to the summons "on any appropriate ground."

Therefore, upon receipt of a summons, you must first determine whether there is "any appropriate ground" available

---
[6] 375 U.S. 440 (1964).

to you upon which to object to producing the records sought in the summons. There have been numerous reasons given by federal courts for refusing to honor an IRS request for enforcement of a summons. A few such reasons are:

1. Improper purpose — bad faith. The summons may not be used to harass a citizen, to exert pressure to settle a dispute, or any other purpose which would indicate the summons is for some other purpose — a bad faith purpose — not authorized by the statute, §7602 of the Code.[7]

2. Unnecessary second examination. Section 7605(b) of the Code provides that a citizen's books and records of account may be examined only one time per taxable year, unless the "secretary or his delegate" notifies the citizen that an additional examination is necessary. Where a person can show that the IRS is conducting an unnecessary second examination without statutory authority, enforcement of the summons could be prevented.[8]

3. Criminal purpose. A summons issued under the authority of §7602 may be used for civil examinations and criminal investigations, provided, in the case of the latter, the IRS — as an agency — has not made a determination to prosecute the taxpayer, and has not completely abandoned the civil aspects of the investigation in favor of the prosecution. See §7602(b) and (c). Where the IRS has abandoned the civil aspects of the case, has made the decision to prosecute the citizen upon completion of the investigation, and is gathering the information for that purpose, the summons may be said to have been issued for an improper purpose.[9]

4. Privileged communications. Communications between an attorney and his client are privileged. That is to say, the attorney cannot be forced, unless the client consents, to disclose the details of his conversations to any other person for any reason. Similarly, documents transmitted to an attorney necessary in obtaining legal advice or assistance are privileged. Consequently, an attorney from whom legal advice was sought and with whom confidential conversations were held and documents transmitted could not be forced to disclose those details to the IRS through the summons process.[10]

---

[7] **United States v. Powell**, 379 U.S. 48, at 58 (1964).
[8] **United States v. London Ins. Agency, Inc.** 76-2 U.S.T.C. 9735 (R.I. 1976); **United States v. Fordin**, 72-2 U.S.T.C. 9618 (N.Y. 1972).
[9] **United States v. LaSalle National Bank**, 437 U.S. 298 (1978).
[10] **Fisher v. United States**, 425 U.S. 391 (1976).

5. Fifth Amendment right against self-incrimination. As stated earlier, the Fifth Amendment has undergone some drastic changes in recent years thanks to the Supreme Court. Vintage court decisions have universally held that a taxpayer need not produce his personal books and records to the IRS if the Fifth Amendment protection is asserted. The Supreme Court, in **United States v. Doe**,[11] held that the books and papers of an individual are not protected by the Fifth Amendment. The court held that the Amendment relates to testimony only, and that when a person takes information from his own head and places it on paper in the form of notes or records, the Fifth Amendment protection dissolves and the IRS may gain access to the records. The court noted, however, that the question of whether the books sought actually exist was a matter of testimony protected by the Amendment, and that without substantive evidence of the existence of the records, the IRS could not gain access to them.

6. Inability to produce. If a person does not have the books and records sought in his possession, care, custody or control, he cannot be ordered to produce them.[12] In fact, **United States v. Curcio** held that once it is established that the individual does not have possession, care, custody or control of records, he may assert the Fifth Amendment privilege as to their location, who does have them, when they were last seen, etc., because these matters are testimonial in nature and the privilege does still apply to testimony.

Whatever the reason applicable to your facts and circumstances, under **Reisman**, you must appear at the time set out in the summons, unless other arrangements are made with the summoning officer. At the appearance, you must be prepared to assert your defenses, giving both the legal reasons and factual basis for the objection. For example, if your assertion is that the Fifth Amendment protects you, you must object to testifying as to the existence of the records, and be prepared to cite your legal authority.

Do not take this as a cue to argue with the summoning agent about the law. This will be unfruitful for both parties. Regardless of what the law is, you will not convince the agent that your view of the law is the correct one. Simply state your position and be done with it.

---

[11] See note 4.
[12] **United States v. Curcio**, 354 U.S. 118 (1957).

THE KNOCK ON THE DOOR 57

If you — either by yourself or in conjunction with your tax counsel — cannot determine that any "appropriate objection," whether stated above or not, applies to your factual situation, you will have to produce the records demanded. Upon producing the records demanded, by sure to have the agent certify in writing that you have complied with the summons in each and every particular.

QUESTION 21
What should I do if the IRS begins a summons enforcement proceeding against me?

You'll know a summons enforcement proceeding has been commenced against you because you will receive by certified mail certain legal documents. Those documents — there'll be three of them — will be entitled 1) Order to Show Cause, 2) Petition to Enforce IRS Summons and 3) Declaration of IRS Agent. Each of these documents has a peculiar posture in the legal arena, but they can be summarized in this fashion:

1. The Order to Show Cause is an order signed by a federal judge. It states that you must appear in court on a certain day, at a given time and place, to "show cause" why you should not be required to deliver the books and records demanded in the summons. The hearing set by the order gives you an opportunity to be heard before being required to disclose your records.

2. The Petition is a formal pleading filed on behalf of the IRS by the United States Attorney, the lawyer for the U.S. government. The Petition states that a summons has been served upon you demanding records, that you have not delivered the records and that the records are necessary to complete the IRS' pending examination.

3. The declaration is a form of affidavit, or sworn statement, executed by the agent who served the summons. It states facts underlying the assertions made in the petition.

Having been served with these documents, the first thing you'll notice after reading the order is that you have a certain, usually very short period of time in which to respond to the documents. You'll then have to actually appear in court a short time after that. As you've probably guessed, if you have a defense to the enforcement of the summons, that defense must be set forth in responsive legal documents which you'll have to file with the court.

58 THE KNOCK ON THE DOOR

A summons enforcement proceeding is a relatively serious matter, especially when the possible ramifications are considered. You will want to consult counsel experienced in the area of summons enforcement with knowledge of the various defenses available, and with the knowledge of the proper procedure to be followed.

Don't choose the first counsel who comes along just because that person happens to have license to practice law. More than one person has hired an attorney on the basis of this kind of recommendation: "My friend is a great divorce lawyer. He can help you with your federal summons enforcement case!" Obviously, an attorney expert in one area of the law is not necessarily expert in every area. Be careful of the counsel you employ to assist you in the matter.

It is possible to represent yourself in a summons enforcement proceeding, provided, however, you have the knowledge necessary to jump through the proper procedural hoops at the right time. The presentation of a defense in this kind of case is not impossible, provided you've done the right preparation. Only you can make the choice of whether to represent yourself or hire experienced counsel, but the decision should be made with dispatch and carried out in earnest.

QUESTION 22
Is a summons enforcement proceeding a criminal case?

No. The difference between a civil case and a criminal case simply is this: In a criminal case, you can go to jail if you lose. You will also be dogged by a criminal record and possibly be placed on probation. Fines and court costs can also be imposed. In a civil case, you stand only to lose that which the government claims they are entitled to in terms of dollars and cents. In the case of the summons enforcement matter, you can only lose your records. That is, you can be forced to turn them over to the IRS.

You must also know that in a civil case the court has contempt power. That means that when a party refuses to obey an order of the court, the court has the power to punish that refusal. This condition is referred to as "contempt of court." Contempt sanctions include imprisonment and fine.

The main difference between civil contempt and criminal imprisonment is that in a civil contempt case the citizen "holds the key to the jail cell." That phrase is used by judges

THE KNOCK ON THE DOOR 59

to illustrate the point that all one need do to resolve the contempt situation — or "purge" himself — is to carry out the order he has refused to obey. This will end the punishment, whatever it is.

QUESTION 23
If I refuse to produce my records, will they always issue a summons?

Like water, the IRS will generally take the path of least resistance when confronted with opposition. In the typical audit situation where a citizen refuses to produce records, it is not always that the IRS will issue summons in an effort to forcibly procure the documents. Because it is much easier for them to simply disallow the claimed deductions, you can expect that this course of action will be the more likely course. However, one can never predict with total accuracy what the IRS will do in a given case. Because they have the power to issue the summons, we should anticipate that such is the course of action they will elect.

QUESTION 24
If I'm summoned to bring in my books, can I get witness fees?

Section 7610 of the Code governs the circumstances under which witness fees will be paid to summoned parties. It states that fees and mileage and costs must be paid to persons summoned to produce records. Section 7610(b) states that payment need not be made to persons having a "proprietary interest" in the books and records required to be produced. That is to say, if the records are your records and your tax liability is under investigation, the statute says you won't get paid.

However, I know of at least one case where an individual required to produce his own records under a summons demanded **and was paid** witnesses fees before going to the IRS office. While this may be the exception and not the rule, it is also true that if you don't ask, you definitely will not receive. All they can say is no.

QUESTION 25
If the IRS can't get records from me, can they go elsewhere to get them?

Section 7602 sets up the rules as to whom a summons may be directed. The statute is very broad in its reach. Strictly speaking, the IRS has the authority to summons any person to give testimony or produce books and records which "may be relevant or material" to the examination.

For example, it is very routine for the IRS, during an audit, to go to the citizen's bank and employer and pull all the records maintained by them. These records are cross-checked with claims made on the tax return, and with the citizen's own records in an effort to detect cheating.

It works this way: The citizen claims income on the return of $25,000. The IRS pulls the bank records which show deposits to the bank account of $40,000. The additional $15,000 is unexplained, so the IRS has a fraud case on their hands.

For some reason, people just generally don't think that the IRS has access to their bank records. Of course, this is not true. Without any knowledge on your part of the rules regarding access to bank records, the IRS could have your records within 30 days of the time they start their effort to get them.

QUESTION 26
What must the IRS do to gain access to my bank records?

First, they must serve a summons on the bank demanding records of your accounts and transactions. They then must wait at least 20 days. Under §7609, if no action is taken by the citizen within that time, the bank must surrender the information.

If you wish to prevent IRS access to the records, you must take the action described in §7609. At the time the summons is issued, you will receive a copy of it and an IRS form outlining your rights under §7609. In a nutshell, they are this:

1. Within 20 days of receiving your copy of the summons directed to the bank, you can file in the federal district court **where the bank is located** a civil action known as a Suit to Quash IRS Summons. This means that you have sued the IRS for an order preventing them from gaining access to the records.

2. You will then go to court to present your legal and factual reasons why the IRS should not be allowed to rummage through your bank account.

After the hearing, the court will decide whether the IRS gets into the accounts or not. Keep in mind that IRS is not at this point after the money in the account. They want only the records in order to "determine your correct tax liability."

Like the summons enforcement case discussed earlier, you will want to make a fast decision as to whether you'll represent yourself or hire experienced counsel. The rules for doing both have already been set out and should be followed.

Another important point on this topic is that the rules outlined here apply only in certain cases. Section 7609 lists the circumstances under which a citizen may file a suit to quash. Generally, it can only be done where the IRS issues a summons to "third party recordkeepers." A third party recordkeeper is defined in §7609(a)(3) as:

1. any bank or savings and loan;
2. any consumer reporting agency;
3. any person extending credit through the use of credit cards;
4. any broker;
5. any attorney;
6. any accountant; or
7. any barter exchange organization.

Only when these organizations are summoned are you entitled to exercise the rights set out in §7609. Any other organization or class of organization is not characterized as a third party recordkeeper and thus, you do not have the right to bring a suit to quash any summons issued to such an organization.

One exception to this rule may exist. In the case of **United States v. New York Telephone Company**,[13] the Second Circuit Court of Appeals ruled that a citizen was entitled to the benefits of §7609 when the IRS summoned the phone company for his telephone records. I have not found any other clear exceptions to the language of §7609(a)(3).

---

[13] 644 F.2d 953 (2nd Cir. 1981).

QUESTION 27
If they can get my records anyway, why shouldn't I just turn them over at the audit?

It is true that if you don't produce the records they ask for, they can get access to the information through third-party sources. They can even get payroll records from employers. At the same time, if you don't produce evidence of deductions, they may well disallow them.

Based upon these facts, the simple answer seems to be just to turn the records over at the audit and save yourself the hassle of having them snoop through your bank and possibly other storehouses of personal data. Simple answers, however, are not always the correct ones. Before the decision to produce or withhold records is made, various factors must be weighed to determine the advisability of any particular course of action.

Some factors which weigh in favor of producing records are:

1. They seek to verify only one or a few **specified items** of deductions on the return. Where items have been selectively picked out of a group, this tends to indicate that a general "fishing expedition" is not in progress.

2. Where only one year is questioned, and not a series of two or more years.

3. Where you've had no prior contact by other divisions of IRS for the same year under audit. This may tend to indicate that the case hasn't been referred to another division for other than civil treatment.

Some factors which weigh against production are:

1. Where the records or testimony are sought by a representative of the Criminal Investigation Division. Under these circumstances, the IRS will only seek to use the data against you in a criminal prosecution.

2. Where they want verification of each and every item on the return, without regard to any particular claim. This may indicate that a general "fishing expedition" is in progress, which may lead beyond a mere audit into a criminal investigation.

The main thing you are concerned with when considering whether or not to produce is the element of self-protection. First blush would seem to indicate that problems begin only if production is refused, but such is not always the case. Careful consideration of all the facts is important.

In one case that I know of, agents appeared at the office of an individual, announced that they were conducting an investigation and asked for all his records. Wanting only to cooperate, he turned over the records initially requested. When asked, he gave full explanations about what kind of bookkeeping techniques he used. One request lead to another, to where the agents spent months going over every entry and demanding explanations. After all his cooperation, the individual was charged with violations of the tax code when the agents discovered errors in his accounting practices.

Examples abound of where the IRS takes innocent statements, made either in writing or in explanation of actions, and uses them against their maker. When you don't know the purpose of the question in the first place, you cannot be sure that the answer won't be used against you, innocent or not.

It should be noted that when it turns out that all questions are indeed asked in a civil context, all records could be produced at a later date when the risk of self-incrimination has been eliminated or substantially diminished. This will be discussed later on.

QUESTION 28
What if I or my counsel cannot get along with the revenue agent?

It is sometimes a problem where the revenue agent is of such a disposition that meaningful cooperation between the agent and the citizen or his representative is impossible. If this situation presents itself, I recommend that a letter be written to the agent's Group Manager, the supervisor directly above the agent.

The letter should set out in detail the nature of the problem and request that the case be assigned to another agent. The more specific you can be as to the nature of the problem, the more likely will be your chances of having the case re-assigned.

If this letter is not successful, a similar request should be made to the District Director, the management official responsible for the district, which in most cases consists of one entire state. The District Director is the highest management official in the state.

64 THE KNOCK ON THE DOOR

QUESTION 29
What kind of records do I need to prove my deductions?
I will classify proof into several areas and discuss the merits of each type of record.

1. First is the most common — the cancelled check. The cancelled check provides positive proof that an amount was paid to a certain person on a certain date. Many times, however, the nature of the payment is vague because the name of the payee doesn't always reflect the precise nature of the payment.

For example, a check made payable to "William Nesmeth" will not necessarily prove the point that Mr. Nesmeth is in fact Dr. Nesmeth and the payment was for medical bills. Still, checks will rarely be contested if, where it's not obvious on the face of the check, the nature of the payment can be fully explained. It is a good idea to use the small space provided on the corner of your check blanks to make a note showing what the payment was for.

2. Second is almost as common — the cash receipt. When payment is made to a person or organization, that person or organization will usually provide a cash receipt. The receipt is valuable evidence since it provides the date of the transaction, the amount, the name of the party to whom the money was paid, and, in the case of businesses, the title of the business. Receipts will often itemize the nature of the payment. This is helpful for businesses wishing to deduct payments for services or products purchased.

The most common problem with the cash receipt is that it is often undated. An undated receipt is worthless, unless by explanation, its date can be fixed. As you may have noticed, where a cash receipt is coupled with a cancelled check, this would provide irrefutable evidence of a payment and the nature thereof. Provided the law allows a deduction for the type of payment evidenced, it would have to be allowed.

3. Third is probably the best record — the year-end statement. Some organizations, such as banks, provide a year-end statement showing, for example, the amount of interest paid during the course of the year. This kind of record can be the best evidence of a payment, since it would include the precise amount of total payments made, the year in which they were paid, to whom and by whom they were paid, and for

THE KNOCK ON THE DOOR 65

what they were paid. With all of this information on one document, no better record can be produced.

To the extent that it is possible, it may be beneficial to ask each organization with whom you've done business to provide such a record. Churches, doctors, mortgage companies, and any other such organizations have the information at their fingertips and can easily provide such documentation. This will make the pangs of an audit far easier to withstand.

4. Fourth is the least known method — the reconstruction. Where you have made payments for which you have none of the first three kinds of records, a reconstruction can be made which can be just as effective. List on paper the approximate dates of the payments, the amounts, the persons to whom paid and what the payment was for. Make a separate sheet for each category of deduction, such as interest, charitable contributions, etc.

When coupled with positive explanation behind each payment, the reconstruction can be as valid any other method of proof. Keep in mind, however, that whether or not a reconstruction will be accepted will depend upon the particular agent. We will discuss later the procedures to follow if any deduction is disallowed, whether or not based upon a reconstruction.

5. Fifth is the least effective — oral testimony. At the audit level, simply testifying that you had made payments of a deductible nature will probably not impress most revenue agents. You will probably hear a response which goes something like this: "Well, Mr. Jones, I'm sure you're telling the truth, but unfortunately, the law does not allow me to accept the deduction unless you have some proof."

On the other hand, testimony can be very valuable as a supplement to the other kinds of proof, especially the reconstruction. It is also possible to sustain a claimed deduction solely on the basis of testimony. We'll discuss that later. You must realize, though, at the audit stage, very few revenue agents will accept the claimed deduction with nothing more than your "good word" that you in fact made the payments.

QUESTION 30
What if I don't have records?

It is not uncommon for people to fail to keep records of certain transactions, or to destroy records after a certain period of time. This presents a problem if called for an audit.

Two things should be done immediately upon notification of an audit. First, begin reconstructions of the items you claimed on your tax returns. These reconstructions should be as thorough as possible. Next, you should contact the persons or firms with whom you've had transactions during the audit year, and ask them to provide you with a copy of a year-end statement for that year.

Organizations such banks, mortgage companies and churches will have no problem complying with this request, but it may take some time. So the sooner you begin the process, the better off you'll be. It may be necessary to postpone your audit conference until such time as the material can be collected. Most revenue agents will not object to postponing audits for a reasonable period of time.

With your reconstructions and year-end statements, you should be able to present an accurate picture of your claimed deductions. Keep in mind that you'll be supplementing your presentation with oral testimony, but oral testimony by itself at the audit stage will not be too impressive.

If, during an audit, you find that you are short of specific records, ask the examiner for additional time in which to gather the needed information. Never take the position — at least initially — that the needed records don't exist. If you don't have them, ask for time to get them. During the interim, you'll be able to get year-end statements, or if no other form of record is available, compile reconstructions.

QUESTION 31
How long should I keep my records?

This question concerns many people, particularly businesses and professionals. The Internal Revenue Code does not specify the length of time which records must be maintained. It does require "taxpayers" to keep records of "income and expenses" for purposes of computing their correct tax liability. Similarly, it does not define what a record is.[14]

---

[14] See §6001.

THE KNOCK ON THE DOOR

An answer to this question will require a look at the statutes of limitation set out in the Code. A statute of limitation is a law which sets a limitation on the period of time in which the IRS may take action with respect to a tax return. The limitation periods differ for varying circumstances.

Since the period of limitation is tied directly to the date of filing the return, we must look at what constitutes the filing of a return. A return is considered filed when:

1. It is mailed by regular mail. When a return is mailed in a timely fashion, it is considered filed timely, regardless of when the IRS receives it. See §7502(a).

2. It is mailed **via** certified or registered mail. The postage receipt for certified or registered mail is evidence of filing. See §7502(c).

3. Under §7503, when the last date for filing falls on a Saturday, Sunday or legal holiday, mailing by the next business day is considered timely filing.

Once it is determined when the return has been filed, the period of limitation begins to run on the next day.

As a general rule, under §6501(a) assessment of any tax must be made within a three-year period beginning with the date a return is filed. Unless the tax is assessed within that three-year period, the IRS is barred from collecting or attempting to collect the tax, either by proceeding in court or by administrative levy. This general rule applies not only to the tax, but to interest and penalties as well.

Based upon this information, we could set as a general rule a three-year retention period for records relating to the typical tax return. You will note that this time frame coincides with the three year "taxpayer profile" called for in the Plan. Still, there are exceptions to this general rule which extend the three-year period. The general exceptions are:

1. Where no return has been filed, or where the IRS asserts that a return is false or fraudulent, there is no period of limitation. Assessment and collection action can be undertaken at any time.

2. Where there has been a substantial omission from a return (i.e. 25% of gross income), the period of limitation is six years. See §6501(e).

3. Where a tax return claims carryback deductions, such as net operating loss carrybacks, or investment tax credit carrybacks, the limitation period for the prior years will remain

68 THE KNOCK ON THE DOOR

open until the expiration of the limitation period for the year of the loss or credit. Example: You file a return in 1984 and claim a net operating loss carryback to 1983. The period of limitation for the 1983 return will remain open as long as the period for 1984 is open, which, under normal circumstances, is three years from the date the 1984 return was filed. The effect, then, is that the 1983 return will be held open for one extra year.

There are certain other, more technical exceptions to the general three-year rule, but the three exceptions delineated above are fair representations of the what the average person need be concerned with.

If, after reviewing all the rules and exceptions to the rules you are still looking for one simple answer to the original question, that answer would probably be that records should be retained for at least six years. The six-year rule would apply to most businesses and individuals.

Specialized businesses and professionals, such as banks, doctors, lawyers, accountants, etc., have record retention rules which are generally set by either state or federal law, or by professional association guidelines. If you fall into the category of a specialized business or profession, you should check with your trade or professional association to discover what the record retention guidelines are.

QUESTION 32
How many times can I be audited for a single year?

The answer is found in §7605(b) of the Code. The law prohibits an "unnecessary examination" and provides that citizens can only be audited once for any one tax year, unless the individual is notified in writing by the IRS that a second examination is necessary.

Once a case is closed, it will not be reopened to make an adjustment **unfavorable** to the individual unless one of three circumstances suggests the need. They are:

1. There is evidence of fraud, concealment, or misrepresentation of a material fact;

2. There was an error made in the prior closing which involved a clearly defined and well established Service position which **existed prior** to the initial closing; or

THE KNOCK ON THE DOOR 69

3. Other circumstances exist which tend to indicate that failure to reopen the case would result in a serious administrative omission.[15]

A case can be reopened to make adjustments **favorable** to the individual without regard to the guidelines described above.

QUESTION 33
When is a case considered closed?

The point at which a case is closed differs depending upon whether the case is an agreed case or an unagreed case. The definition of an agreed case, as you might imagine, is one where the individual agrees with any proposed adjustments presented after the examination. An unagreed case is one in which the individual does not accept the findings of the examination.

An agreed case is considered closed when, after the examination, the individual is notified in writing of the proposed changes in the tax return, or the return is accepted as filed. He must of course accept any proposed changes. An unagreed case will not be considered closed until after the individual has exhausted his appeal rights.

QUESTION 34
What will happen when the audit is complete?

After any face-to-face meetings with the revenue agent have been completed and the agent has the material in his hands upon which to base his findings (or is satisfied that it can't be had), a report will be written. This report is called an examination report and may say one of two things.

If there are no changes to the return, then the report will consist of simply one letter informing you that your return has been "accepted as filed" and that no changes are intended.

If changes are made, such as the disallowance of deductions, the specific deductions which are challenged will be set out in the report together with an explanation as to why they have been disallowed. The agent will then recompute the tax liability, add in interest and penalties and ask for payment of the total amount shown.

---

[15] These guidelines are found in the Federal Tax Regulations, at §601.105(g).

70 THE KNOCK ON THE DOOR

QUESTION 35
Must I always pay the amount they say I owe?
When you receive your examination report, you will find enclosed a Form 870, Waiver. The letter will instruct you to sign the form if you do not wish to contest the adjustments. If you sign the form, the adjustments will become final and the amount shown will become immediately due and payable; you will have given up your right to appeal the changes.

The letter transmitting the examination report will be either a so-called fifteen-day or a thirty-day letter. A fifteen-day letter will give you fifteen days in which to submit additional information to the revenue agent, or to make another appointment to discuss the proposed changes in the return. The thirty-day letter states that you have thirty days in which to request a hearing with a member of the Appeals Office.

On the basis of this information, then, if you wish to settle the case, the 870 should be executed and returned to the agent. You will receive a bill for the tax in due course, which will have to be paid.

If you disagree with the proposed changes, **do not sign the 870**. Rather, you must request a hearing before the Appeals Office within the 30 day period set out in the letter. You do not have to pay the tax before receiving your hearing with the Appeals Office.

QUESTION 36
How do I make an appeal to the Appeals Office?
Appeals within the IRS are handled by the Regional Director of Appeals. The Appeals Office has personnel in the district and they will act as hearing officers in appeals cases. As part of the standard package of enclosures sent with a thirty-day letter, you will receive a copy of IRS Publication 5.

Publication 5, Appeal Rights and Preparation of Protests for Unagreed Cases, sets out in detail the manner in which a case is brought before the Regional Director of Appeals for a hearing with an Appeals Officer. The procedure can be summarized in this fashion:

For cases where the amount in controversy is in excess of $2,500, a written protest letter must be sent to the district director. The office address of the director will be shown plainly on the thirty-day letter. The written protest must contain, in this order:

THE KNOCK ON THE DOOR

1. A statement that you want to appeal the findings of the examiner to the Appeals Office;
2. Your name and address;
3. The date and symbols of the letter transmitting the proposed adjustments which you are contesting;
4. The tax years involved;
5. An itemized schedule of the adjustments with which you do not agree;
6. A statement of facts supporting your position; and
7. A statement outlining the law upon which you rely.

Your letter must also contain a statement to the effect that the facts set out in your letter are, "under penalty of perjury, true and correct to the best of your knowledge." The letter must be signed and mailed to the district director within the thirty-day period.

Where the case involves an amount in controversy less than $2,500, an appeal can be requested without having to meet all of the requirements set out above.

QUESTION 37
Can IRS send me a bill without giving me an opportunity to appeal?

It is very common for IRS Service Centers to send computer generated recomputation notices. A "recomp notice," obviously a computer printout, is a bill for taxes with no clear explanation as to why it's being sent. The notice demands that you pay the amount shown, with interest, immediately. We have already briefly discussed this kind of notice in Question 3.

Although you are not told this fact in the letter, you have the right to object to the payment of the tax if you do so in the proper fashion. Upon receipt of a recomp notice, you have, according to §6213(b) of the Code, 60 days in which to object in writing to paying the tax. There is no specified form that the objection must take.

Upon receipt of the objection, the IRS is obligated to abate the tax. If they feel that they are entitled to collect the amount, they must proceed by sending you a Notice of Deficiency. A Notice of Deficiency will be discussed at Questions 67-69.

The recomp notice seems to be gaining popularity with the IRS. With the installation of the Automated Collection Division, a completely computer-operated system of tax collection, these notices are sent with startling regularity. Because there is no explanation with the letter clarifying why your tax has been increased, the tendency of people is to call or write Automated Collection for an explanation. This is a waste of time. The telephone operator will just say "You owe this amount, and you'd better pay it." No positive information is ever received.

In the meantime, the 60-day time period provided by statute expires and the tax is then collectable. I believe that through the use of the recomp notice, the IRS will attempt to collect tens of millions of dollars by "nickel-diming" the American public to death. This is a most effective way in which to collect more money with less effort as called for in the Plan, don't you agree? Just send somebody a bill for $850 in taxes and don't explain where it came from.

Of course, much of the money demanded through this process is not legally owed, but because they will do nothing to explain your rights to you, they'll eventually get it. Once you pay such a bill, you are marked as an easy collection target. Then every time the IRS gets the bug to go on a collection rampage, whose name do you suppose they'll call up on the computer?

Watch for the recomp notice and remember you must object to the tax within 60 days. Simply asking for an explanation will do nothing but permit the time to lapse.

QUESTION 38
Can I negotiate a settlement with the examiner?

We have all heard advise to the effect of "Make them an offer. Never pay what they ask for. They'll probably settle for less." This suggestion is not altogether incorrect, but if you wish to attempt to negotiate a settlement with the revenue agent, first understand what it is you are negotiating.

If your approach is: "The bill is $2,500, I'll give you $1,500 to settle the whole case," the agent will respond with: "Well, Mr. Jones, the bill is $2,500. That's your correct tax liability. We can't change that. You have to pay your correct tax liability. There's nothing I can do."

As you can see, this angle has gotten you nowhere. Realize that the **tax**, a figure arrived at by applying your taxable income to the tax tables, is not negotiable. What is negotiable, however, is the amount of **taxable income** you actually have.

THE KNOCK ON THE DOOR

Since taxable income is not computed on the basis of statutes carved in stone, but rather on the individual facts of each case **vis-a-vis** itemized deductions, negotiating the itemized deductions can usually prove very beneficial.

For example, suppose you have claimed a home-office expense of $1,000, and that expense was arrived at on the basis of the proposition that 20% of your home was used exclusively for business. After examination, the IRS reduces the deduction to 10%, or $500. You are then billed for the additional tax. Rather than arguing about the additional tax, which is carved in stone, argue about the 10% home office figure, which is not. If, by negotiating the expense, you persuade the agent to allow 15% of your home as an office, you have just saved yourself 25% of the additional tax demanded.

This technique is the only way to successfully negotiate with the IRS. The method can be used not only at the examination level but also at the Appeals level and beyond.

QUESTION 39
What penalties can be added to a tax bill?

Penalties are added to tax bills as a matter of course. There are several **ad valorem**[16] civil penalties which come into play in the typical tax audit situation. You should be aware of what they are.

The first is the negligence penalty. Under §6653(a), a penalty equal to 5 percent of the underpayment of tax is added for negligence or intentional disregard of rules and regulations. This penalty will routinely be added to any underpayment of tax. The citizen bears the burden to prove that the penalty is inappropriate and must demonstrate that it should not be added.

The Code does not define the term negligence, but the courts have said that "negligence is lack of due care or failure to do what a reasonable and ordinarily prudent person would do under the circumstances."[17] Evidence which would tend to vitiate negligent conduct on your part would be necessary to defeat the negligence penalty.

Such evidence could include proof that you simply made a mistake. You cannot be held liable for the penalty if your

---
[16] An **ad valorem** penalty is one which is based upon a percentage of the tax found to be due.
[17] **Marcello v. Commissioner**, 380 F.2d 509 (5th Cir. 1967).

conduct was based upon an honest mistake in your understanding of the law, or if your action was taken in good faith and was based upon reasonable grounds.[18]

Reliance upon a competent and fully informed tax advisor or return preparer has also been held as grounds for not including the negligence penalty. If it can be shown that your return was prepared by a competent preparer, or that you relied completely on the advice of tax counsel, the negligence penalty should be lifted.[19]

The second area of primary concern is the delinquency penalty. The penalty is imposed in accordance with §6651 of the Code for any of three reasons: 1) failure to file a return in a timely manner, 2) failure to pay the tax, and 3) failure to pay an assessed tax. The difference between items two and three is simple. Item two applies to the tax shown due on a tax return, which should be paid at the time of filing the return. Item 3 relates to a notice and demand for additional tax assessed after an examination, or by means of a recomp.

The delinquency penalty is computed differently depending upon whether the penalty is assessed for failure to file or failure to pay. However, the maximum penalty in either case is 25 percent. The penalty is computed on the amount of the deficiency in tax only, not on the entire tax liability.

The only basis for escaping the imposition of the delinquency penalty is "due to reasonable cause and not willful neglect." See 6651(a)(1) & (2). Internal Revenue Regulations[20] provide that if you wish to defeat the delinquency penalty, you "must make an affirmative showing of all facts alleged as a reasonable cause." More simply put, you have to prove that the delinquency penalty is inappropriate in your case after consideration of all the facts and circumstances.

The Internal Revenue Manual gives examples of what they would consider reasonable cause.[21] They are:

1. A return mailed in time but returned for insufficient postage;
2. A return filed in time but with the wrong IRS office;

---

[18] **Scott v. Commissioner**, 61 T.C. 654 (1974).
[19] **Industrial Valley Bank & Trust Co. v. Commissioner**, 66 T.C. 272 (1976).
[20] Rev. Reg. §301.6651-1(c)(1).
[21] The IR Manual is the operating instruction book used by IRS personnel. The section we refer to here is IRM 4562.2(1)(a) through (h).

THE KNOCK ON THE DOOR 75

    3. Erroneous information from an IRS employee, such as Taxpayer Assistance personnel;
    4. Death or illness of the individual, or a person in his immediate family;
    5. Unavoidable absence of the individual;
    6. Destruction of business or records by fire or some other casualty;
    7. A request for the proper return blanks not timely provided by IRS;
    8. A request for information and assistance by appearing at an IRS office, but through no fault of your own, you are unable to meet with IRS personnel.

Other grounds for not imposing the delinquency penalties have been recognized by the courts, and they include, as mentioned earlier, reliance upon a professional, competent tax advisor or return preparer. When a person relies completely upon such professional advice, and the advice turns out to be wrong, the individual cannot be held responsible for the penalty, especially where the question is one which the individual would not normally be aware.[22]

One further ground recognized by the regulation as justifying a failure to impose the delinquency penalty is "if the taxpayer exercised ordinary business care and prudence and was nevertheless unable" to meet the obligation to file or pay. Just what constitutes "ordinary business care and prudence" is not defined in the regulation, and can only be answered by looking at all the facts and circumstances of each case. In any event, you must prove that you exercised such care and prudence.

The next penalty we'll discuss grows out of §6654 of the Code, and is a penalty for underpayment of estimated tax by individuals. The penalty is the same as the rate of interest currently charged by the Code for underpayments of tax. See §6621, and the next Question. The penalty is based upon two essential elements. The first is amount of the underpayment and the second is the duration of the underpayment.

To determine the underpayment, simply take the amount of tax shown due on the return, or, if no return was filed, the amount of tax determined due after examination, and subtract the amount of installments made. An installment would be

---

[22] **Hardwood Lumber & Mining Co. v. Commissioner**, 178 F.2d 771 (2nd Cir. 1950) and **Coldwater Seafood Corp. v. Commissioner**, 69 T.C. 966 (1978).

money paid through wage withholding or some other method of installment payment. Eighty percent of the difference is the amount of underpayment.

The duration of the underpayment runs from the date the installments were supposed to have been made, to the earlier of: 1) the final date for payment of the total tax (usually April 15th) or 2) the date the final payment is actually made.

Section 6654(d) sets out four conditions under which the failure to pay estimated tax penalty will **not** be imposed. They can be summarized in this fashion:

1. If the estimated tax you paid in the present year equals or exceeds the total tax paid in the previous year, the penalty will not apply. §6654(d)(16).

2. The penalty will not apply if your installments were based upon last year's income, but calculated using this year's tax rates and exemptions. §6654(d)(4).

3. The penalty will be avoided if you've paid installments equal to 80 percent of the tax due on your annual income. §6654(d)(2).

4. The penalty will not apply if your installments equal 90 percent of the tax due of your actual income, computed on a quarterly basis. §6654(d)(3).

The penalty for underpayment, unless one of the four exceptions delineated above is shown to exist, is mandatory. There is no statutory provision for "good cause" or "lack of willful neglect." If you've underpaid during the course of the year, an installment penalty under §6654 will be demanded, based upon the amount and the duration of the underpayment.

The last **ad valorem** penalty we will discuss here is referred to as the civil fraud penalty, imposed under §6653(b). The penalty is equal to 50 percent of the underpayment if "any part of an underpayment. . .is due to fraud." The civil fraud penalty is not a criminal sanction. That is to say, if found guilty of civil fraud, you will not face a jail sentence, or fines in the context of a criminal case. The exposure under §6653(b) is limited to the addition of 50 percent of the underpayment of tax.

In order to sustain the 50 percent penalty, the Commissioner must show with "clear and convincing evidence" that the citizen has been guilty of fraud with intent to evade tax.[23] The

---

[23] See §7454(a).

THE KNOCK ON THE DOOR

individual, on the other hand, will have to show that there has been no underpayment of tax; that the Commissioner's determination of a tax deficiency is erroneous. If there is no deficiency, of course there can be no penalty. Such is the case with not only this penalty, but with each of the **ad valorem** penalties we've discussed.

Fraud and what constitutes fraudulent actions have been much litigated areas over the past several decades. From among this mountain of case authority come definitions and guidelines which are helpful in our analysis. One leading case[24] has defined fraud as "conduct, the likely effect of which would be to mislead or conceal." Another[25] has said that the "voluntary, intentional violation of a known legal duty" is evidence from which fraud could be inferred.

The allegation of fraud is a very serious one, and the cases plainly indicate that fraud involves more than a mere failure to carry out a duty. A finding of fraud requires that one carry out specific acts — as distinguished from failures to act — the effect of which is to deceive or mislead.[26] Mere negligence or even gross negligence, while resulting in an underpayment, does not rise to the level of fraud. To act fraudulently, one must act with a specific mindset to do what he knows the law forbids. Failures to act are not sufficient; there must be evidence of affirmative acts to sustain the finding of fraud.

Specific acts which have been said in the past to constitute evidence of fraud are:

1. Deliberate failure to keep adequate books and records, or the maintenance of false books and records, or the maintenance of a duplicate set of books and records.[27]

2. Excessive and unjustified claims of deductions, especially where personal expenses are claimed as business expenses.[28]

3. A consistent pattern of understating income with no justifiable explanation. One isolated instance of underpayment is not sufficient. There must be a pattern to indicate that the ommissions were intentional.[29]

4. Evidence of fraud can also be inferred from the individual's conduct during the course of the investigation. For

---

[24] **Spies v. United States**, 317 U.S. 492 (1943).
[25] **United States v. Pomponio**, 429 U.S. 10 (1976).
[26] **Mitchell v. Commissioner**, 118 F.2d 308 (5th Cir. 1941).
[27] **Otsuki v. Commissioner**, 53 T.C. 96 (1969).
[28] **Habersham-Berg v. Commissioner**, 78 T.C. 304 (1982).
[29] **Lollis v. Commissioner**, 595 F.2d 1189 (9th Cir. 1979).

78 THE KNOCK ON THE DOOR

example, false statements made to investigators, attempts to hide assets, false records supplied to investigators, and destruction of records have been held to be evidence of fraud.[30]

5. Using covert means to conceal assets, such as use of secret bank accounts, placing assets in the name of others or in fictitious names, or the extensive use of currency.[31]

On the other side of the coin, defenses to a fraud assertion which have vindicated people in the past fall into the same general categories as those we've already discussed. The primary defense would be lack of specific intent to evade the payment of the tax. Where it can be shown that the individual lacked the intent to break the law, but was merely mistaken or even negligent in his conduct, the fraud penalty will not attach.[32]

Similarly, complete reliance upon expert advice by an ignorant individual will result in the fraud penalty being vitiated.[33] This rule also holds where the individual passes on to an expert accountant or bookkeeper his books and records for return preparation, and the expert makes an error in the final return.[34]

Many times, the court will look to the attributes of the person in question in determining whether the fraud penalty is appropriate. An unsophisticated person without knowledge or training to equip him to make a correct decision will not be held liable for the penalty, absent evidence of specific intent to commit a fraudulent act.[35] A non-expert will not be held accountable for the fraud penalty where the issues involve complex questions with which the ordinary person would not be expected to be familiar.[36]

Whether or not the fraud penalty will be imposed will be determined by a Judge of the Tax Court after a trial has been held. At the trial, each party will be permitted to present evidence tending to support his claim. The IRS will of course present evidence that the underpayment was deliberate, willful and intentional, and the citizen will attempt to convince the court otherwise.

---

[30] **Estate of Beck**, 56 T.C. 291 (1971); **United States v. Beacon Brass Co.**, 344 U.S. 43 (1954).
[31] **Spies**, (see note 24); **Furnish v. Commissioner**, 262 F.2d 727 (9th Cir. 1958).
[32] **United States v. Bishop**, 412 U.S. 346 (1973); **United States v. Dahlstrom**, 713 F.2d 1423 (9th Cir. 1983).
[33] **Durovic v. Commissioner**, 54 T.C. 1354 (1970).
[34] **Cohen v. Commissioner**, 27 T.C. 221 (1956).
[35] **Iley v. Commissioner**, 19 T.C. 631 (1952); **Marinzulich v. Commissioner**, 31 T.C. 487 (1958).
[36] **United States v. Garber**, 589 F.2d 843 (5th Cir. 1979).

THE KNOCK ON THE DOOR 79

Each penalty we have discussed here may be negotiated with the IRS at any level of the examination or appeal. Certain evidence you have may convince the IRS to drop a claim of fraud or negligence or some other penalty before it goes to the level of the Tax Court.

QUESTION 40
When will interest be included in a tax bill?

Interest is always added to any unpaid balance. The interest is computed from the date of the notice and demand for payment, and no interest is due if the tax is paid within 10 days of the date of the notice and demand. See §6601(e). The rate of interest is set by statute (§6621), and will run until the tax and penalties are paid in full.

The statute ties the rate of interest to the prime rate, which is the rate commerical banks will charge their best corporate customers for loans. To reduce a complex computation to simple terms, the rate can change twice a year depending upon the current prime rate of interest.

The Tax Equity and Fiscal Responsibility Act of 1982 substantially changed the manner in which interest is computed. Prior to the act, IRS used the simple interest method. Under this method, you would not find yourself paying interest on interest. Effective January 1, 1983, interest is compounded daily, with the result being that you could pay interest on interest. See §6622.

Given the fact that interest is compounded daily, and the rate can change as many as two times per year,[37] it is impossible to manually compute to the dollar what interest will be charged on a given amount due for a given period of time. IRS uses its computers to make the computations.

QUESTION 41
Am I responsible for mistakes made by my return perparer?

The obligation to file a correct income tax return is a non-delegable responsibility. That is to say, you cannot push on to someone else the duty of filing your income tax return, even if that person is a professional return preparer. The law does recognize limitations to this rule which we have just discussed

---

[37] Since February 1, 1978, the rate charged by the IRS has changed eight times.

in Question 39, but as a general matter, you and you alone are held accountable for what goes into your tax return.

Similarly, where you are represented by counsel in a tax matter, you **will** be held accountable for statements and representations made to the IRS by your counsel. This is called the doctrine of vicarious liability. It means simply that you — as the principal — are bound by the acts of your agent — the tax preparer or counsel. For these reasons, you would do well to carefully choose and then carefully monitor the actions and statements your counsel or preparer makes on your behalf. You, not he, will be the one to pay the piper in the end.

QUESTION 42
If you were to diagram the various levels of the IRS that we've discussed so far, what would it look like?

Beginning with the audit, the progression of a case through the IRS to this point in our discussion, is shown in Figure 1.

Figure One
Progression of Tax Audit

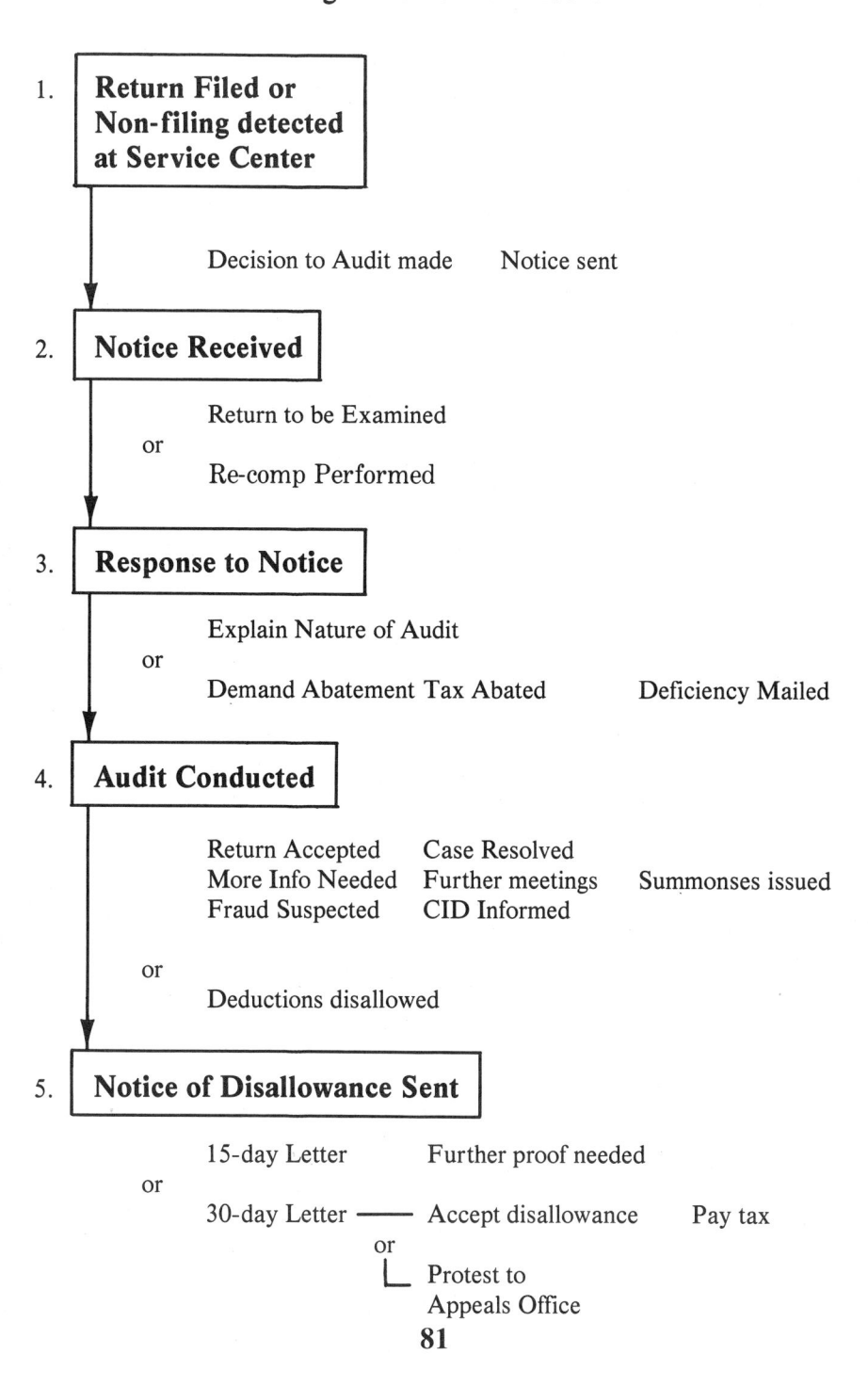

1. **Return Filed or Non-filing detected at Service Center**

   Decision to Audit made   Notice sent

2. **Notice Received**

   or   Return to be Examined
        Re-comp Performed

3. **Response to Notice**

   or   Explain Nature of Audit
        Demand Abatement   Tax Abated   Deficiency Mailed

4. **Audit Conducted**

   Return Accepted   Case Resolved
   More Info Needed   Further meetings   Summonses issued
   Fraud Suspected   CID Informed

   or   Deductions disallowed

5. **Notice of Disallowance Sent**

   or   15-day Letter   Further proof needed
        30-day Letter ——— Accept disallowance   Pay tax
                          or
                          └ Protest to Appeals Office

Chapter Two
AVENUES OF HOPE
Questions Relating to Appeals

Background to this Chapter —
The Administrative Procedures Act of 1946 was the beginning of a blatent departure from Constitutional standards, and was a major step in an evolutionary process which has transformed our legal system. Prior to the Act, the powers of the legislative, executive and judicial branches of government were completely separate. No branch had the power or authority to perform the functions or duties of the other.

We were all taught that the legislative branch of government — the Congress — writes laws; the judicial branch — our federal courts — judge the laws written by Congress; and the executive branch carries out the functions of government enumerated in the Constitution.

In theory, the separation of the powers of government into these branches prevents any one branch from becoming autonomous. Our Founding Fathers reasoned that such a system would prevent the United States from becoming the kind of despotism which had plagued the American Colonies before the war for independence and which was present in England for centuries before that.

The significance of the Administrative Procedures Act can be summarized this way: Federal administrative agencies, such as the Internal Revenue Service, have been given the power to 1) write their own laws which take the form of federal regulations that are binding to the same effect as statutes written by Congress. They 2) judge their own laws through the Appeals Office and through the United States Tax Court, an administrative tribunal. And 3) they enforce their own laws through their administrative police force, which takes two forms. One is the Criminal Investigation Division, which is responsible to investigate all possible violations of the federal tax laws.[1] The other is the Collection Division,[2] which is responsible to collect all taxes lawfully assessed and owing.

At this stage of our examination, we will focus upon the Appeals Office, what it is and how it functions. Keep in mind that the Appeals Office is found within the administrative

---
[1] CID will be discussed in Chapter Four.
[2] To be discussed in Chapter Three.

scheme of things. That is to say, although it is completely independent of the Examination Division, it is nevertheless part and parcel of the Internal Revenue Service.

The Appeals Office represents the single level of appeal within the IRS. After any review at the Appeals level has been unfavorably exhausted, the case may be pursued through the court system in one of only two ways. The first way is to proceed to the United States Tax Court, which operates under the Executive Department of government.

The Tax Court began as the Board of Tax Appeals in 1924. It was part of the Executive Branch, functioning within the IRS as the Appeals Division presently does. In 1942, the name was changed to the Tax Court of the United States, but continued to function within the IRS as an agency of the Executive Department.

With the Tax Reform Act of 1969, the name and status of the court was changed. Since, it has been referred to as the United States Tax Court. Its status was altered from that of an administrative tribunal under the Executive Branch to a so-called Article I court, functioning under the Executive Branch of government.

If all of this seems confusing and pointless, consider the significance to be simply this: Congress proposed and the Supreme Court approved of creating a "court" with the power to resolve disputes between a citizen and the government, but in which the citizen would not be afforded traditional Constitutional rights, such as the right to jury trial.[3]

While the proposal had floated around Congress and the IRS for a number of years, the move wasn't made until 1969. Apparently it took that long for Congress to work up the nerve to create a court wherein the American people didn't enjoy all of their Constitutional rights.

The second way to prosecute an appeal is to, under special circumstances to be discussed later, proceed to the United States District Court. This court is a court of law established under Article III of the United States Constitution. In the district court, all Constitutional rights are supposed to be jealously guarded by the judges. This would include the right to a jury trial.

---

[3] **Philips v. Commissioner**, 283 U.S. 589 (1931).

The Appeals Office, because it is separate and distinct from the Examination Division, and because it is the one and final appellate authority within the IRS itself, has the power to resolve any disputed liability for taxes and penalties in most cases. The general area of jurisdiction, or authority, which the Appeals Office has is in cases of income, estate and gift taxes, and penalty and employment taxes, where no assessment[4] has yet been made.

QUESTION 43
Why must I be concerned about appeals?

You're probably asking yourself: "If all goes well at the audit level, why should I worry about appealing my case?" To answer this question, please be cognizant of the overall purpose of the Plan. You'll recall that the main goal is to collect more money with less effort. Consequently, we can no longer expect the IRS to simply roll over in audit situations.

For years, the American people have been playing the so-called "audit lottery." Audit lottery is a game wherein the players claim questionable deductions on their tax returns in the hopes that theirs will **not** be one of the relatively few selected for audit. In audit lottery, the player bets on the odds. To a large degree, they have been successful.

Now, however, with the increased ability to audit tax returns and the goal of auditing everybody one way or the other, the IRS can be expected to begin playing "appeal lottery." Appeal lottery is a game wherein tax examiners will make questionable rulings in audit situations believing that most citizens, intimidated by the system, will simply pay the additional amount rather than appeal for a just ruling.

The sad truth is that most probably will simply pay, partly due to intimidation and partly because they can't afford the legal talent needed to fight and don't know how to do it themselves.

QUESTION 44
When can an appeal be taken?

Appeals in unagreed cases can be taken where the IRS asserts a liability for income, estate, gift, or employment taxes and related penalties. An unagreed case, as we have already

---

[4] The term assessment and its meaning is discussed in Chapter 3 relating to Collection.

learned, is one in which the IRS and the citizen cannot come to terms on the extent of the liability.

The time to file the appeal is crucial and is governed by regulation. As we have already pointed out, the appeal steps are clearly set out in IRS Publication 5, which fully explains the applicable regulations.

The general rule is that you have 30 days from the date of notification of any change in your tax liability by the Examination Division in which to appeal that proposal to the Appeals Office. Adherence to the time limitations set by the IRS is always a prerequisite to getting justice. If you ignore time deadlines, you can expect the IRS — and, if you get that far — the courts, to ignore your cries for justice.

QUESTION 45
Can I always appeal my case?

Changes proposed by the Examination Division are always appealable to the Appeals Office. However, you will give up the right to appeal your case if you sign a Waiver, Form 870, and consent to assessment of the tax. If this is done, you may pursue other avenues which will result in a review of the assessment, but do not necessarily involve an appeal to the Appeals Office.

Provided you continue to disagree with the IRS and do not waive your rights to have the matter reviewed, you will be entitled to a review before the tax becomes irrevocably fixed and payable.

QUESTION 46
Does the tax have to be paid before I can Appeal?

That depends upon the kind of tax involved. One class of tax is subject to deficiency procedures, meaning it need not be paid before appeal. Another class of tax is not subject to deficiency procedures, meaning it must be paid before appeal.

A tax is "assessed" when it is recorded in the IRS office as due and owing, and can be collected with all of the collection tools available to the government. A tax which is not assessed cannot lawfully be collected. Ordinarily, before any tax can be assessed, you must be given the right and opportunity to argue over its propriety.

In matters of personal or corporate income taxes, employment taxes, excise and gift taxes, and most penalties, before the tax can become assessed, you must be given an opportunity to contest it.

In the vast majority of cases, you will receive a notice indicating that IRS intends to change your tax liability by increasing it. Before it can be officially increased, you have the opportunity to appeal the decision before they can legally collect the increased liability, interest or penalties. The procedures which relate to pre-assessment review are referred to as deficiency procedures.

In a few rare cases, the tax can be assessed without regard to the deficiency procedures. The cases in which deficiency procedures are not used involve certain penalties and the so-called jeopardy assessment under §§6861 and 6862. These will be discussed in Question 86.

QUESTION 47
Must I take my case to the Appeals Office before going to court?

From a strict Constitutional perspective, perhaps the most oppressive contingency of the Administrative Procedures Act is the portion which requires a claimant to "exhaust all available administrative remedies" before pursuing his claim in the federal court system. What this means in simple terms is that if you have a disagreement with the IRS, or any other federal administrative agency, before that disagreement can be brought before any court for a binding judicial resolution, you must first use the administrative avenues of appeal available to you within the agency in question.

The Constitutional affront inherent in this rule occurs where the courts refuse to take jurisdiction or authority to hear a case when administrative remedies have not been exhausted. A seasoned practitioner is well aware of the rule requiring the use and exhaustion of administrative procedures, and is knowledgeable as to how that is best accomplished.

The average man on the street, however, is usually not aware of these subtle nuances in the law. His first inclination is to bring the dispute before a court of law in an effort to get justice. When he does, he is told by the judge that his case cannot even be heard, much less settled. This causes much consternation.

In the meantime, because he has bypassed the administrative process and has gone directly to court, he may well have

AVENUES OF HOPE

waived his right to go back to the administrative agency due to the time constraints on filing a case there. The result: The citizen is deprived of justice simply due to ignorance — a reason which should never figure into the dispensation of justice in a Constitutional Republic.

For those cases which are presented at the administrative level, we find the problem of subjectivity. That is, the agency is not inclined to overturn its own decisions, even though made at a lower level. The result is that after lengthy and sometimes costly administrative appeals have been exhausted, you're still at the point where you were when the process began.

Still, under the present structure, you must always exhaust all available administrative procedures within the IRS, including taking your case through the Appeals Office, before you can pursue the matter into the courts. If you fail to do this, you may well give up all rights of appeal, whether administrative or judicial.

QUESTION 48
Do I have a choice of where to appeal my case?

When a case comes out of Examination as an unagreed case, the next level of appeal is the Appeals Office. In every case where the IRS demands additional dollars in taxes or penalties, there are two ultimate avenues of pursuit available.

For purposes of simplicity, we will call the first and most common avenue the pre-payment avenue, because you do not have to pay the tax before embarking upon it. The pre-payment avenue will lead you eventually to the United States Tax Court, which is an administrative tribunal established under the Executive Department of Government. Therefore, we will refer to the pre-payment avenue as the "administrative route."

The next available route we will call the post-payment route, because in order to pursue this course, the taxes, interest and penalties will have to be first paid in full. The post-payment route will eventually lead to the United States District Court, which is a court established under Article III of the United States Constitution, which created the Judicial Branch of Government. This form of appeal will be known as the "judicial route."

Thus, in each case where IRS seeks additional taxes from you, the choice you have is to either follow the pre-payment or post-payment remedies available to you.

In either the pre-payment or post-payment forum, you will have to use the Appeals Office before the matter can be brought to the next highest level. The Appeals Office is the final authority within the IRS relating to tax liabilities, and the forum must be utilized and exhausted before going on.

QUESTION 49
What's the difference between the administrative and judicial appeal routes?

The most obvious difference between the two has been mentioned; in order to pursue the judicial route, you must first pay the tax. A claim for refund must then be filed and denied. Once the claim is denied, you can file a lawsuit in the United States District Court for your state and district.

The administrative route does not require payment of the tax. Before the tax is assessed, you may, if the Appeals Office continues to maintain that you owe additional taxes, petition the United States Tax Court for a determination of your liability without paying the tax. While the case is pending in the Tax Court, the IRS cannot lawfully move to collect any of the alleged tax liability. See §6213.

QUESTION 50
Which court is more desirable, the Tax Court or the District Court?

There are pros and cons to each court, and whether to journey one way or the other depends upon the facts and circumstances of each case. If we list the positive and negative attributes of each court, you can determine for yourself, given the facts and circumstances of your case, which route is the most desirable.

Tax Court - positive features —

1. Citizen may enter Tax Court without first paying the tax.

2. While the case is pending, the IRS cannot attempt to collect the tax.

3. When you represent yourself, judges tend to relax the rules of procedure just a bit, making it less formal.

4. In special cases, called Small Tax Cases, a simplified process is available which completely relaxes the rules.

5. The rules governing the court are relatively simple and straightforward.

Tax Court - negative features —

1. You have no right to a jury trial because the court is an administrative tribunal established under the Executive Department of government, not a judicial court established under the Judicial Branch. In fact, no Constitutional rights typically observed in a court must be afforded in this forum.

2. Interest on the unpaid tax claimed will continue to accrue at rates established by §6621(b). See Question 40.

3. In Small Tax Cases, if you lose the case, you have no right to appeal that decision to a higher court. This is not true of regular tax cases, however. These may be appealed.

4. The percentage of citizen wins in the Tax Court is very small. Some attribute this to the fact that most, if not all of the Tax Court Judges have had extensive careers with the IRS at one point in their lives.

5. Your tax trial will be held only in a designated Tax Court city. You can select the city nearest you for the trial, but the Tax Court — based in Washington — does not travel to every city in the country.

6. You can be penalized up to $5,000 for instituting a "frivolous" Tax Court case primarily for purposes of delay. See §6673.

District Court — positive features —

1. The District Court may properly be characterized as a "real court," wherein you enjoy all of your Constitutional rights, most particularly the right to a jury trial when the amount in controversy exceeds $20.[5]

2. The District Court sits in every major city in the country. Consequently, you will not have to travel far — if at all — to have your trial.

3. Because of pre-payment, interest stops accumulating against you, and if you are successful, the IRS will have to pay interest to you on the amount you have recovered from them.

4. All cases are appealable to a higher court, regardless of their nature.

5. If successful, under certain circumstances you could recover from the United States your costs of maintaining the suit for refund.

---

[5] See Constitution, Amendment 7.

District Court — negative features —
1. The tax, interest and penalties must be paid in full before a refund suit can be commenced.
2. The rules of procedure are more complex and burdensome.
3. Judges tend to be quite determined to enforce the rules, making the presentations more formal.
4. If the court finds that your suit was "frivolous," you may be made to pay the costs and attorney's fees incurred by the government.[6]

QUESTION 51
Where is my administrative appeal filed?

The administrative appeal, filed in the form of a written protest[7], goes to the Office of Regional Director of Appeals. The address of this office will be provided you by the local IRS district office upon request. After your protest is received, you will be notified of the date of your appeals hearing, which will be referred to as an "appeals conference."

QUESTION 52
What must I do to take a judicial appeal?

At any time before a petition with the United States Tax Court is filed, you may elect to pursue the avenue of judicial appeal. This is done by first paying the tax, interest and penalties which IRS claims to be due. There is no need to pay the tax "under protest," to preserve your right to file a claim for refund, but it would be wise not to sign any waiver forms in connection with paying the tax.

After paying the tax in full, a claim for refund must be filed. The time for filing the claim is set by statute and must not be ignored. Section 6511(a) provides that you have three years from the date of filing the initial return in which to file the claim for refund. If no return was filed, you have two years from the date the tax was paid. If you miss these time limitations, you will forfeit your right to claim a refund of your money.

---

[6] See 28 USC §2412.
[7] We have already discussed the written protest. See Question 36. Also, as we have said, IRS Publication 5 describes the procedure in detail.

QUESTION 53
How is a claim for refund filed?

The claim for refund should be filed with the IRS office where the tax was paid. If the tax was mailed to the Service Center, then so too should the claim for refund. Keep in mind that the IRS will be very strict and unforgiving where time constraints are concerned.

Federal regulations dictate the form and substance of the claim for refund. Generally, a claim is made on Form 1040X, Amended Federal Income Tax Return, or Form 843, Claim for Refund. A more informal demand for refund can be made by just submitting the claim on typewritten paper, so long as it conforms in substance to the requirements of the regulations.

The regulations require that claims set forth in detail each reason why a claim for refund is made, and facts which support the claim. The Commissioner must be able to glean, by reading the claim, exactly what the nature of your claim is, and upon what grounds the claim is based.[8]

Your claim must also state the amount you have determined as an overpayment of tax, and whether the amount should be refunded to you, or applied as a credit to next year's tax liability. The rule of thumb to follow in making your claim is this: The claim must make full and complete disclosure of all the facts, and must give reasons why you feel you are entitled to the refund or credit. Anything less is not sufficient.[9]

One final, very important rule to be aware of regarding the substance of claims for refund is this: Only those issues which are raised in the claim for refund may be raised in any subsequent suit for refund. Therefore, you must be very careful to clearly state all reasons you know of which entitle you to the refund or credit. If you fail to raise any issue, you will be prohibited from raising that issue later in court.

QUESTION 54
When can I file my suit for refund?

Section 7422 of the Code gives the district courts jurisdiction, or authority to hear suits for refund only after all administrative remedies have been exhausted. This means that before the suit can be filed, the claim for refund must be filed and denied.

---

[8] See. Rev. Reg. 301.6402-2.
[9] See also Rev. Reg. 31.6402-3.

92 AVENUES OF HOPE

Section 6532(a) establishes the time in which a suit for refund can be filed. It states that a suit cannot be filed **before** the expiration of six months from the date the claim is submitted, or **after** two years from the date the IRS denies the claim.

To clarify, you must give the IRS at least six months in which to rule on your claim. Before they do so, they are likely to hold an appeals conference to give you an opportunity to provide proof of the nature of your claim. Whether or not a hearing is granted, you will have to wait at least six months before any further action can be taken. If no written word ever comes, this failure to respond may, after six months has lapsed, be treated as a denial of your claim and a suit may be commenced in the district court.

Always remember: Failure to exhaust administrative remedies will result in your case being dismissed without a ruling on its merits.

QUESTION 55
Will I get a hearing in my administrative appeal?

If an administrative, rather than judicial appeal is taken, the chances are very likely that you will be given a hearing before the Appeals Office. The hearing, called an Appeals conference, will be held at the IRS Office, and will be presided over by an Appeals Officer.

The Appeals Officer is a specially trained representative with the power to settle the case, and you can expect a conference to be held within about 90 days of the date your written protest or claim for refund is received.

QUESTION 56
What procedures are followed at an appeals conference?

An appeals conference is a very informal meeting. The participants usually consist only of the Appeals Officer and the citizen whose case is in question. Other participants may include the citizen's counsel, who may be an attorney or accountant, or other qualified counsel, and possibly a representative of the Office of District Counsel. District Counsel is the staff of attorneys who represent the IRS in Tax Court matters. They are of course employed by the government, but work exclusively for the IRS.

The conference, as the name suggests, takes place in a conference room, over a table, and not in a courtroom. There are no formal rules which are observed, and there is no formal procedure which is followed in the conduct of Appeals conferences. You have a full opportunity to present any material which you believe will benefit your case.

QUESTION 57
Can I have counsel with me at the conference?

You always have the right to counsel present with you at any stage of an IRS proceeding, whether administrative or judicial. Counsel may consist of an attorney, an accountant, an agent enrolled to practice before the IRS, or a practitioner admitted to practice before the United States Tax Court. Treasury Publication 230 sets out the details of who may represent others before the IRS.

QUESTION 58
Can I have witnesses present at the conference?

The purpose of the conference is to develop the facts and argue the law governing the issues in question. To aid you in presenting a complete picture of the facts, you may very well wish to have witnesses present. Any person who can provide testimony which will demonstrate to the Appeals Officer the nature and truthfulness of your claim would be helpful as a witness.

For example, suppose you have claimed a charitable contribution for money given to a church, and the IRS disallowed this deduction because you failed to provide a receipt or cancelled check showing the amount paid. At your Appeals conference, you may wish to bring as a witness the treasurer of the organization to which the money was given. That person could testify, from the records of the organization which he was responsible to keep, that you in fact gave a specified amount of money to the organization in a given year. The presentation of these facts will go along toward convincing the Appeals Officer that you are entitled to the deduction which was disallowed by the examining agent.

In any given dispute, you will have to develop the facts for the Appeals Officer. The use of witnesses at the conference will provide great assistance in doing this. One need not worry about the proper way to "question" the witness. Since the conference is very informal, the witness can simply tell his story to the Appeals Officer.

QUESTION 59
How will I be expected to present my case?
   As I have stated, the Appeals conference is very informal, but you will be expected to accomplish certain things. You have to demonstrate the facts of your case, and the law which governs the issue, to the satisfaction of the Appeals Officer before he will rule in your favor. My experience has shown that most Appeals Officers will explain the nature of the meeting and what they want you to do.
   Generally, they will just ask you to show them what documentary evidence, if any, you have on the question. Here is where you will produce receipts or cancelled checks, or any other documents which you have to prove your point. You can also present any testimony, that is oral explanation, on the issue. You as the taxpayer may provide testimony, and any witnesses you have may also provide testimony.
   Similarly, you should give a statement of the law of your case, and why you feel that the law has been complied with in your case.

QUESTION 60
What is the difference between law and fact?
   It is very important for you to understand the difference between these two terms if you are to be successful in your case at any stage.
   The term "fact" applies to historical events. When asked for a statement of facts, or testimony on the facts, you must confine your remarks to that which took place in a historical context. Examples of facts include the amount of a payment, the date of a payment, the person to whom the payment was made, reasons why the payment was made, the nature of services received in exchange for the payment, etc. As you see, all of these matters relate only to events or circumstances which have a place in history.
   Facts are not to be confused with opinion, conjecture, or some other subjective explanation of what happened or why it happened. Facts should be thought of only as history.
   The law, on the other hand, should be thought of as the principles or rules which govern your subject matter. When presenting the law, you will look to the statutes which Congress has written, the regulations promulgated by the IRS and the decisions of the various courts which interpret the former. All these taken together amount to the law of the case.

Any presentation must take into account both the law and the facts. You should be prepared to paint a picture of the facts through documents and testimony, and argue the law from the statutes, regulations and court decisions.

QUESTION 61
How are the facts best presented?
The facts are best presented in a systematized format designed to conform to the requirements of the statute in question. To illustrate, let's take the very simple example of interest deductions. Section 163(a) of the Code provides that:

> "There shall be allowed as a deduction all interest paid or accrued within the taxable year on indebtedness."

The statute goes on to discuss interest in other contexts, such as interest on investment indebtedness. For purposes of this illustration, we will confine ourselves to subsection (a), as quoted above.

This statute, as does every statute, contains separate elements, or subparts of the whole. The facts must demonstrate that each separate element has been met in order to be entitled to the deduction. The elements of §163 are:
1. That interest was paid;
2. That it was paid during the taxable year in question; and
3. That it was paid on indebtedness.

Once that you have identified each of the elements which comprise the statute, you must now organize your facts so as to be able to prove that each of the separate elements are present and have been met in your case.

Referring to our example, you'll first need proof to establish that interest was in fact paid. You will need either a cancelled check, a receipt, oral testimony from yourself or from some witness who can verify payment, or any combination of these or other methods of proof.

Next, you'll have to show that it was paid during the year in question. The dates of your cancelled checks or receipts could satisfy this need.

And lastly, you must prove that the interest was on indebtedness. This element could be shown by producing a copy of the installment or other contract which you signed promising to pay an amount of money, with interest, over a period of time. Satisfaction of the elements of the statute is referred to as your "burden of proof."

By organizing your facts in this way, you will be will assured that you have not left out an important element of your case. The rule is that if you fail to prove any one separate element, you will fail in your entire case. Therefore, you must be careful to first identify what each element is, and then gather and organize your facts to meet each and every element.

QUESTION 62
How is the law best presented?

As mentioned earlier, law — or, governing principles — takes the form of statutes, or acts of Congress, regulations promulgated by the IRS, and the court decisions which interpret them.

The law is best presented on an issue-by-issue basis. That is to say, where you have more than one character of deduction in dispute, present law on each issue after you have presented the facts on that issue. In this way, your presentation will retain continuity and you personally will not become lost in the shuffle. More importantly, when organized and presented this way, you will be sure not to skip a segment of any one issue, whether it be a law or fact segment.

It is always helpful to present court decisions as part of your package on the law. Court decisions will interpret the statutes and regulations in question, and provide insight as to how they are to be applied. Court decisions supporting the kind of interpretation you are attempting to advance will be very helpful in persuading the Appeals Officer to your point of view.

One thing to keep in mind when in the Appeals conference is that Appeals Officers, unlike revenue agents, are very much aware of the law, both in the context of statutes and court decisions. This can be both a detriment and benefit for you. It can be detrimental if you have not done the background homework on your issue. You may well be bluffed if you cannot point to specific authority which supports your position.

On the other hand, you may not have to go to great lengths in the argument of your case if your issue is one with which the Appeals Officer is well familiar. Under such circumstances, he may be quick to agree with your position, whereas the revenue agent would not bend on the subject.

Actual copies of the applicable statutes, regulations and court decisions are available at any law library. You will have to do the research necessary to find the particular items you need. Once you have found them, take photocopies along with you to the appeals conference. This way, you will not have to rely upon memory when it comes to discussing the language of the law. You can refer to your actual copy and read directly from it where appropriate.

It is also a very good idea to prepare for the IRS' side of the case before your conference. Anticipate what the officer will have to say in opposition to your claims, and stand ready to refute those propositions.

QUESTION 63
Will I receive only one Appeals conference?
If progress is being made in the case, you will receive as many conferences as is necessary to amicably resolve the issues. If, for example, you don't have all the evidence in your possession to satisfy your burden of proof, a second meeting can be set at which the material will be presented once you've had a chance to gather and organize it.

If you feel that further conferences would be helpful, ask the Appeals Officer to schedule another.

QUESTION 64
What basis is used by Appeals Officers to make decisions?
The main factor that Appeals Officers use in making decisions is the probability or likelihood of success at trial. When the law and facts are such that the Appeals Officer believes that you cannot convince a judge that you are entitled to what you're claiming, he will not allow your claim.

On the other hand, where you have shown sufficient law and facts to cast a substantial doubt in the mind of the officer as to whether the IRS would be successful at trial, then you will probably win your case at the Appeals level.

QUESTION 65
Can I negotiate with the Appeals Officer?
Absolutely. Since the Appeals Officer has the complete authority to make a decision on the case, he is the ideal person to negotiate with. Keep in mind the rules of negotiation which we have already discussed. See Question 38. Do not attempt to

negotiate the tax liability. All negotiations must center upon the deduction in question. Question 38 gives a detailed example of what I mean.

Another important thing to remember when negotiating with Appeals is that since all matters are decided primarily upon the basis of probability of success, it is a good idea to talk in terms of what the "evidence at trial would show." So, for example, if you were negotiating the deductibility of the interest in our earlier example, (Question 61), you could summarize your position as follows:

"Mr. Appeals Officer, the evidence at trial in this case would be that $2,250 was paid by me in the taxable year 1985. The evidence will also show that the interest was paid to the ABC Credit Agency for a loan they made to me. So as you can see, all of the elements of a §163(a) deduction will be shown at the trial of this case."

What this does is to put into prospective for the officer just exactly what the evidence at the trial will be. This helps you to lead the officer to the conclusion that you have satisfactorily met your burden of proof on the particular question. The same approach should be taken with the law.

Once this is done, you are in a position to request full allowance of the particular deduction. If the officer doesn't agree that you have proven the deduction, or believes that you aren't entitled to the entire amount you've claimed, you will begin to negotiate to reach an acceptable settlement.

One further thing should be noted here. It is the natural tendency of all of us to attempt to encourage a settlement by discussing the "nuisance value" of a case; that is, the costs of litigation that will be saved by settling the case without the need of a trial.

Any offer to settle will not be considered if it is premised upon the costs of litigation. As far as the government is concerned, they don't care about the costs of litigation. In negotiations, you will have to present such facts and law as will raise a doubt in the mind of the officer as to the IRS' ability to win the case in court.

QUESTION 66
How are cases settled at the Appeals level?
Once an agreement is reached between the Appeals Officer and the citizen, a settlement agreement will be written up. The

agreement will show a recomputation of the tax based upon the accords reached at the conference.

Once the recomputation is done, the parties must sign the agreement in order for it to be binding. The form most commonly used by the Appeals Office to record such agreements is Form 870-AD. The form states that the citizen accepts the liability, if any, and agrees that "no claim for refund or credit shall be filed or prosecuted" for the years in question. The effect of this form is to make the agreement final and binding upon the citizen.

The interesting thing about Form 870-AD is that **it is not binding** upon the IRS. The only agreements which are recognized by the courts as binding upon the IRS are formal closing agreements made in accordance with §7121. Under §7121, the IRS is authorized to enter into the closing agreement and, when approved, it is "final and conclusive" on the question of your tax liability for that year.

Unlike with the 870-AD Form, the IRS cannot reopen a case after it's been settled with a formal closing agreement. The agreement may not be modified and it cannot be set aside or annulled in any legal proceeding. Based upon this knowledge, it may be desirable for you always to insist on a formal closing agreement once a settlement has been reached. This will prevent the IRS from reneging on the agreement once it has been struck.

QUESTION 67
What will happen if we cannot reach an agreement?

If an agreement cannot be reached, the Appeals Office will cause a notice of deficiency to be mailed to the citizen. The notice of deficiency states that the IRS has determined that there is a deficiency, or underpayment in your income tax liability for a given year.

At the point of receiving the notice of deficiency, you have two courses of action available to you. First, you can pay the tax they say is due. Having paid the tax, you can file a claim for refund. If the claim is denied, as it very well could be, you can file a suit in the district court demanding a refund of the money paid. Keep in mind all of the rules that we have laid out in this Chapter for the filing of claims for refund, particularly the time constraints.

If you decide that you cannot pay the tax they say is due, or determine that you would rather pursue your case in the Tax Court, then you must file a petition with the United States Tax Court in Washington, D.C. The petition must be filed within 90 days of the date stamped on the notice of deficiency.

The 90-day period does not begin running on the day you receive the letter. It commences on the date stamped on the face of the letter. This is very important because if your petition is filed late, the Tax Court will not be able to hear your case. The result: You lose by default and will have to pay the full amount of the tax, interest and penalty. Then your only option will be to file a claim for refund.

It is very important to understand that the collection of federal income tax liabilities is unlike the collection of any other debt in the United States. Under ordinary circumstances where it is claimed that Party A owes Party B a sum of money, Party B must file a lawsuit and prove the debt exists before he can collect one penny of the amount claimed. **It is the opposite** with the IRS.

When they assert a deficiency, **you must file the suit** and prove you don't owe the money in order to prevent them from collecting it. If you do not take action to resolve the matter of liability within the 90-day period, either by petitioning the Tax Court or by paying the tax, the amount claimed on the notice of deficiency will become assessed and fully collectable by the IRS with all of the enforced collection tools available to them.

As we shall see later, the IRS' collection arsenal is very formidable. Therefore, when faced with a notice of deficiency, it behooves you to make up your mind presently and proceed without delay in the manner you have chosen.

QUESTION 68
How long will it take the notice of deficiency to issue?

You can usually expect the notice of deficiency will take about 60 to 90 days to reach you. This time would be computed from the day it has become apparent that you will not reach a settlement with the Appeals Office.

QUESTION 69
Can I appeal the notice of deficiency?

Appeal of the notice of deficiency involves petitioning the United States Tax Court within 90 days of the date stamped on the face of the notice. The Tax Court makes its home in Washington, D.C. Their address is 400 Second Street, Northwest, Washington, D.C. 20217. The court has available a rule book which will help you in the prosecution of your Tax Court case. You must obtain a copy of it and read the rules if you intend to be successful in your case.

One further important observation on the notice of deficiency. The Tax Court is very serious about adhering to the 90-day time deadline. The deadline is set by Congress and cannot be changed. See §6213. If you wish to perfect any appeal to the Tax Court, you must see that the petition is in the hands of the Clerk of Court before the expiration of the 90-day period.

QUESTION 70
Can I change from the Tax Court to the District Court, or vise-versa?
No. Remember that the Tax Court is available only to those who do not wish to first pay the tax. The district court is available only after you've paid the tax in full and had a claim for refund denied. Once a petition is filed with the Tax Court, you will not be able to get your case into the district court. Judges like to say "you can't have two bites of the apple."

On the other hand, if you've paid the tax in full, the Tax Court has no authority to hear the case. Authority to do so would be vested in the district court after your claim for refund is denied.

QUESTION 71
Who will represent the IRS in court?
In Tax Court, the IRS will always be represented by District Counsel. Those lawyers work exclusively for the IRS and their primary duties are the handling of Tax Court cases. They are government attorneys, but don't work in any other area of the government.

In district court, the IRS will be represented by either the local United States Attorney's Office, or by a lawyer from the Justice Department out of Washington, D.C. The Justice Department is broken into various divisions, one of which is the Tax Division. Lawyers from the Tax Division will most likely find themselves defending the government in tax refund cases.

QUESTION 72
What kind of trial can I expect?

In either the Tax Court or the district court, you can expect a trial consisting of an opportunity to call witnesses in your own behalf, and to cross-examine those witnesses called by the government. You will have a chance to develop the facts for the court, and to submit a written statement of the applicable law. Through this process, the law and the facts are put before the court for resolution.

In the district court, you have the right to a jury trial. So unlike in the Tax Court, a jury of your peers will decide the facts of your case. In Tax Court, a judge will decide all matters of both law and fact.

QUESTION 73
How long will it take the court to decide my case?

I have seen Tax Court judges take a year or more to reach a decision. In other cases, decisions of the Court come very quickly. In either the Tax Court or the district court, you can expect a final decision to take at least 90 days to six months.

QUESTION 74
Can I appeal the decision of the court?

Decisions of the district court, and decisions of the Tax Court in regular cases can be appealed to the United States Court of Appeals for your circuit. The Court of Appeals is a court established under Article III of the Constitution and reviews decisions of the two lower courts we've been discussing.

Small Tax Cases cannot be appealed. Before you file your petition with the Tax Court, make the decision as to whether you want your case designated as a Small Tax Case. There are simplified procedures available for the so-called "S" cases which sometimes make them more attractive, but you cannot appeal the decision of the court in "S" cases.

You are not required to designate your case as an "S" case. It is purely optional. Be sure to weigh all of the positive and negative attributes before electing "S" status.

QUESTION 75
What exactly is a Small Tax Case?

In cases where the disputed amount is less than $10,000, the Tax Court rules allow you to designate your case as a Small Tax Case. As we have said, a small case is entitled to special treatment, which includes the use of simplified procedures. The downside to an "S" case is that it cannot be appealed. Also, you will not have the opportunity to file with the court a written statement of the law and facts.

If you have erroneously designated your case as an "S" case and wish to change it, or wish to have a regular tax case proceed as an "S" case, this can be accomplished by making a request of the court to redesignate your case.

QUESTION 76
When do I appeal the decision of the court?

If, after reading the court's final opinion, you find that you wish to take an appeal, you have 90 days from the date of that opinion in which to file a notice of appeal. The notice is filed with the clerk of the court which issued the order, and notifies all parties that an appeal to the Court of Appeals is being executed.

The appeal of cases is governed by the Federal Rules of Appellate Procedure, and provision for the notice of appeal is made in the Tax Court rule book, as well as the rules for the district courts. No effort should be made to proceed in any court without first reading the rules of that court. This includes the Court of Appeals.

QUESTION 77
If you were to diagram the various courts that we've just discussed, what would it look like?

A diagram of the federal courts we have been discussing is shown in Figure 2.

Figure Two
Progression of Case Through Appeals and Courts

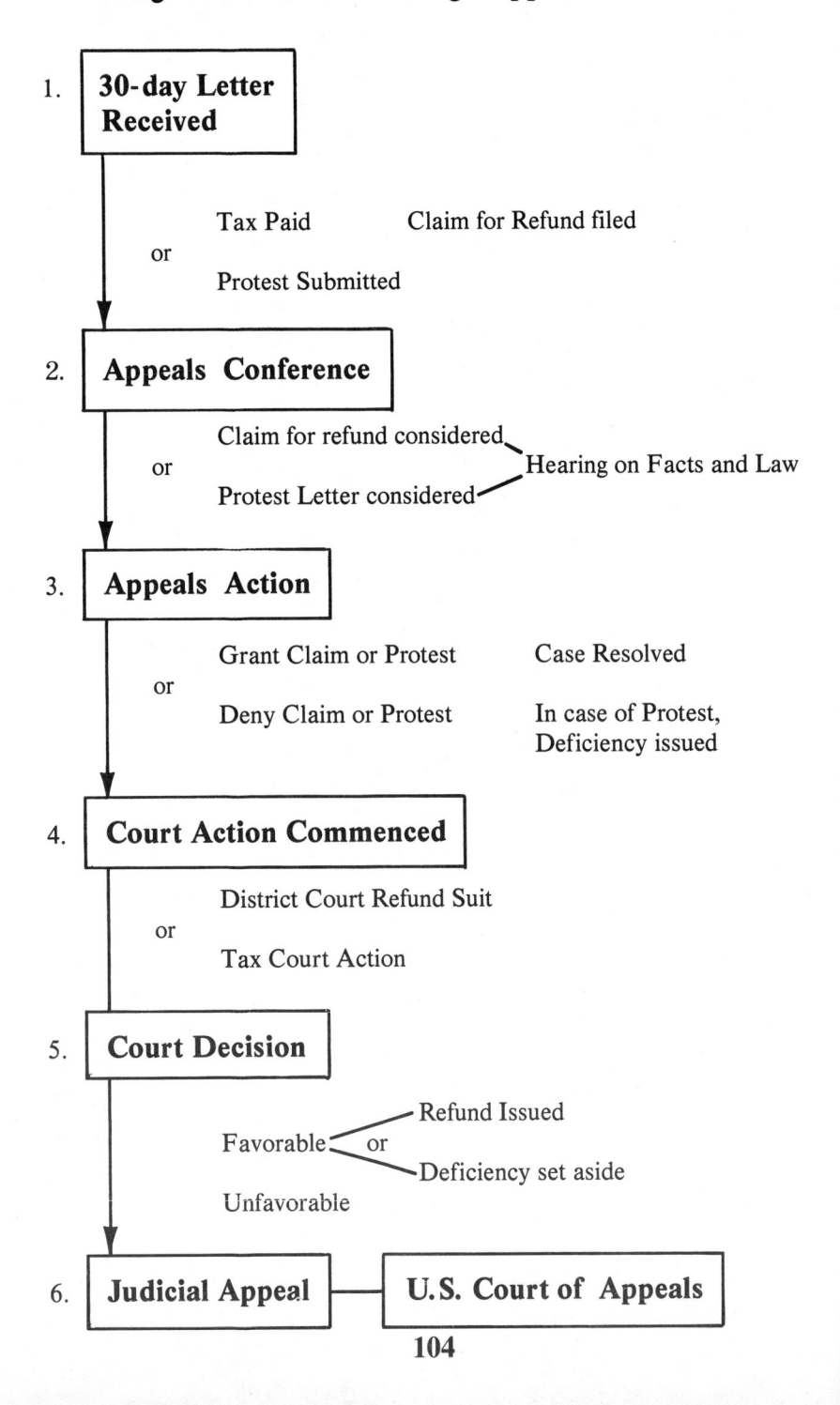

1. **30-day Letter Received**

   or Tax Paid   Claim for Refund filed
       Protest Submitted

2. **Appeals Conference**

   or Claim for refund considered
       Protest Letter considered   Hearing on Facts and Law

3. **Appeals Action**

   or Grant Claim or Protest   Case Resolved
       Deny Claim or Protest   In case of Protest, Deficiency issued

4. **Court Action Commenced**

   or District Court Refund Suit
       Tax Court Action

5. **Court Decision**

   Favorable or Refund Issued
                  Deficiency set aside
   Unfavorable

6. **Judicial Appeal** — **U.S. Court of Appeals**

Chapter Three
YOUR WORST FEARS
Questions Relating to Collections

Background to this Chapter —
The Collection Division and its personnel should be thought of the as the collection agency for the United States Government. Revenue Officers, those within the IRS working expressly in the Collection Division, have the exclusive responsibility to collect unpaid taxes, or, in IRS vernacular, "process inventory."

Until 1984, most collection activity centered in the local district, where teams of revenue officers worked under the direction of group managers to handle the "inventory" within that district. In 1984, as we have already learned from the the Strategic Plan, 21 Automated Collection sites came "on line." Now, much of the collection activity is generated from and directed by the Automated Collection site with jurisdiction over your state.

Automated Collection is your worst nightmare personified. We have always feared the day when the local department store or telephone company would send a computer bill for $1,000,000, and because the entire system was computerized, nobody would be able to correct or even recognize the mistake. This is precisely the case with Automated Collection.

They send out computerized notices which demand payment of taxes, interest and penalties. They don't explain where the figures came from, or why your tax has been increased; they simply demand full payment within 10 days, otherwise "enforced collection action will be taken." What's worse, it is totally futile to correspond with Automated Collection, as everything is handled by computers. You'll simply receive another copy of the original letter which caused all the concern in the first place.

Why not call the toll-free number they provide, you ask. You might as well call the Iranian Embassy and ask them to help with your problem. The "operators" at the other end are capable of only one thing: Punching your Social Security number into the computer and telling you what the written statement has already told you. "You owe X dollars in taxes, interest and penalties and you had better pay — or else." How they were figured? What they are for? Why all the penalties? Nobody seems to know. They just want the money — now.

One case comes to mind which graphically illustrates the frustrations which one can encounter when dealing with the impersonal Automated Collection. The man — an airline pilot — was in the habit, as were most of his colleagues, of deducting certain educational expenses every year. The IRS disallowed certain of these deductions on a nationwide basis. The Airline Pilots Association, the pilot's union, sponsored a case to the United States Tax Court in which many pilots had joined. The suit challenged the IRS' actions and sought a judgment permitting the pilots to deduct the expenses.

The claims in question were made on a 1978 income tax return. They were disallowed in 1980, and unfortunately, the Tax Court ruled against the pilots in 1982. In the summer of 1982, our pilot paid his tax liability, which amounted to approximately $2,500. Having done so, he forgot all about the matter and went on about the business of living.

In 1984, just a little over two years after having paid the tax in full, he began receiving notices from Automated Collection, stating that his 1978 tax liability hadn't been satisfied and that he owed $2,500.00. They said that if the amount wasn't paid immediately, "enforced collection action would be taken."

Knowing that the tax had been paid, he simply sent the IRS a pleasant letter pointing out the fact that they probably had overlooked his payment. For their convenience, he enclosed copies of the cancelled checks to prove he had fulfilled his responsibility.

A few months later, he received another letter from Automated Collection. It — like the first letter — stated that taxes for 1978 were due and owing, and that they had better be paid. This time, our pilot got on the phone. Using the toll free number, he called Denver — the facility whose address was on the letters he received — intending to get to the bottom of the misunderstanding.

While on the phone with IRS personnel, he was finally able to get somebody to recognize that, yes, an error had been made. But if he would just send another copy of his cancelled checks (the first copy had been lost apparently), the discrepancy could be cleared up.

Faithfully, he mailed a second copy of the cancelled checks with a cover letter reciting the details of the conversation.

This, he was sure, would end the problem. It didn't. About a month later, he received another threatening notice and then, much to his bewilderment, a lien was filed on all of his property. The lien came at a most inopportune time as he was just then attempting to sell his house.

After recovering from the shock of the lien, he mailed a third copy of the checks, and a second copy of the just-mentioned letter, to Denver. No response. In the meantime, the lien prevented sale of the house, which in turn prevented closing on a second house on which he and his wife had signed a purchase agreement. The improper tax lien had so completely stirred up their lives that the effect was to leave their affairs much like articles found on the sale table at a clothing discount store.

He finally surrendered his efforts to communicate with Automated Collection and began to communicate with the local United States District Court. A lawsuit was filed which demanded that the lien be removed. An attorney from the Department of Justice was assigned to the case, and after several months of legal fencing the case was resolved. The lien was lifted and things got back to normal.

In retrospect, we find that dealing with Collection in the ordinary fashion we deal with others is not sufficient. When the IRS gets it into their heads that you owe taxes, they will undertake to collect them. Your only salvation will be to know exactly what they can and cannot legally collect, and the circumstances under which it may be collected.

QUESTION 78
Why should I be concerned about "enforced collection?" I pay my taxes.
If the story we have just related doesn't sufficiently answer the question, consider this: The message communicated by the Strategic Plan was that the IRS has declared war on, and leveled its collection guns at you, the average American. We have shown that the goals of increased collection cannot be carried out against the so-called Big Three — organized crime, corporations and tax shelter investors — because these groups have the resources to tie up the machine, rendering it exceedingly difficult for collection efforts to be cost effective.

You, on the other hand, are viewed as defenseless. You probably can't afford high-powered lawyers and accountants to put the IRS through their paces. Moreover, when faced with a bill for $500 or $1,000, you are likely to just pay it without protest "because it's cheaper then fighting." The result is that increased dollars are collected with little or no expenditure of funds — the quintessence of cost-effective collection.

Whether or not you pay your taxes is not the question. The pilot and countless others like him paid their taxes too. The system came down upon him — either knowingly or unknowingly — believing that he was a source of easy money. As it turned out, he wasn't. But that is not to say they won't consider you a source of easy money. The fact is, the Plan indicates that they have placed you in such a category. The only question left now is whether you can deal with the attack when it comes.

QUESTION 79
Who collects money for the IRS?

The Collection Division does all of the actual collection of unpaid taxes. They should be thought of as existing at two separate levels.

The first level is the Service Center level. At the Service Center, we find the Collection Branch of the Compliance Division. They are responsible to send out the computerized notices under the heading of Automated Collection. While the physical location of the various Automated Collection sites — there are 21 — do not coincide with the various Service Centers, they are under the general direction of the Service Center.

The second level is found at the district level, under the authority of the District Director. There you'll find both the field and office branches of the Collection Division. The personnel staffing these branches are referred to as revenue officers, and their duty is to collect unpaid taxes in the cases which are assigned to them.

To get a better feel of where Collection comes into play, consider this progression: In the typical case, we begin with the filing of a tax return. The return is then audited by the Examination Division. After the audit has been completed, the examiner makes a demand for additional taxes. The citizen appeals the demand. The appeal goes to an Appeals Officer where one or more hearings on the matter are held. If Appeals rules against the citizen, he has the choice of pursuing the matter in the District Court or the Tax Court. Since the District Court alternative can only be pursued **after** the tax is paid, Collection will not figure into a refund case.

Collection will come into the act when the Tax Court has ruled against the citizen. Once the Tax Court has ruled, a tax can lawfully be assessed and, hence, collected. The case will be assigned to the Collection Division and enforced collection steps will be taken if full, prompt payment is not made.

QUESTION 80
When will I be contacted by Collection?

If your case follows the normal progression which I have just outlined, you won't be contacted by Collection until after the Tax Court has ruled against you. As the law presently stands, the IRS cannot make any effort to collect the tax when a case is pending in Tax Court. Code §6213 acts as a kind of injunction against this conduct. However, once the Tax Court rules, the tax is legally collectable, even though you may have taken an appeal to the United States Court of Appeals.

I said this is the "normal" progression. Recent history has shown that the IRS is becoming increasingly "abnormal" where their collection practices are concerned. I attribute this to the self-professed autonomy of Automated Collections and the stated, overall purpose of the Plan. More and more I am finding that collection functions do not follow the prescribed course. Attempts by the IRS to collect taxes for which there has been no lawful assessment are increasing with each passing day.

These efforts, not unlike the pilot's case, follow a general pattern. They begin with a notice from Automated Collection. The notice could come anytime and relate to any year. There is no way of pin-pointing just how a given year is selected. The notice will tell you that taxes are due and owing and must be paid. Then, after a series of several such notices, a lien will be filed with the county you live in. Later, a wage levy could be placed against your paycheck.

On the basis of this history, and the indications that Collection is becoming more and more wild in its efforts, we could draw the very reasonable conclusion that collection action could be undertaken at any time with regard to any year, even if your case is in Tax Court and the Court has yet

110 YOUR WORST FEARS

to rule. Whether any unlawful collection action will be successful is entirely up to you.

QUESTION 81
Will I always be audited before I am sent a bill?

If you are thinking of an audit in the sense of sitting down with a revenue agent and showing receipts and cancelled checks for each and every payment you've made during a particular year, the answer is no. Such an examination is not the only kind through which people are put. See Question 3.

The recomputation letter discussed in Question 3 is the result of a perfunctory audit — one which takes place at the Service Center and which consists only of a review of the figures on the tax return. Therefore, do not assume that you will have to undergo an actual examination of your books and records before the IRS will mail you a bill.

As I have indicated, the frequency in which the "recomp" letters are being mailed increases with each day. The chances of your receiving such a bill without undergoing an audit have gone up just in the time it took you to read the answer to this question.

QUESTION 82
What if I get a bill for taxes I don't think I owe?

Before any action is taken in response to an apparent bill from the IRS, you must first determine that it is in fact a bill. A bill takes the form of a one-page letter which will always have the language "request for payment," or "our records show a balance of X dollars on your income tax," or "we have previously written you about the Federal tax shown below. It is overdue. . ." This language plainly indicates that the correspondence is a bill. It will also be an obvious computer print-out.

Do not confuse a tax bill with a proposed assessment. You will recall from the previous Chapters that after the completion of an audit, the IRS will send a 30-day letter which details the proposed changes made in your tax liability. This letter will contain a final tally of the taxes, interest and penalties, and will ask for payment, but it is not a bill. It is a 30-day letter which can be appealed.

Similarly, at the conclusion of an unsuccessful appeal, the Appeals Office will mail a statutory notice of deficiency. This will also tally the taxes, interest and penalties which they claim you owe, and will ask for payment, but it is not a bill. It can be appealed to the Tax Court if a petition is filed within 90 days of the date of the notice.

Once you have determined that the correspondence is in fact a bill — it demands immediate payment of the tax and threatens "enforced collection" if not paid — then you must determine whether you are lawfully responsible to pay the bill.

If you have gone through Tax Court and lost, the tax has been assessed and you will be responsible to pay it. Also, if you have received a notice of deficiency and did not petition the Tax Court within the prescribed 90-day grace period, the tax shown on the 90-day letter has been assessed against you, and you have given up your right to appeal to the Tax Court.

Finally, if you have filed a federal income tax return of some kind to which you signed your name, but have not paid the tax shown on the form as due, then you will be responsible to pay that tax.

On the other hand, if your case is pending in the Tax Court, or if you have not been afforded the appeal rights available within the IRS, then the IRS has no lawful right to collect any tax.

If the IRS demands payment of money when your case is before the Tax Court and the Court has yet to rule, you would want to write a letter pointing out the applicable language of §6213(a).

Section 6213(a) establishes the 90-day time period for petitioning the Tax Court. It provides that an assessment cannot take place, and no action to collect the tax can be undertaken, until the "notice has been mailed to the taxpayer, nor until the expiration of such 90-day or 150-day[1] period, as the case may be, nor if a petition has been filed with the Tax Court, until the decision of the Tax Court has become final.***"

Your letter would be sent to the address shown on the demand for payment, and should include all relevant information about your Tax Court case, such as the date your petition was filed, the docket number, and so on. This will enable Collection officers to verify the existence of your case. Any further effort at collection should then cease. If further

---

[1] Persons living outside the United States have 150 days in which to petition the Tax Court.

collection attempts are made, appropriate action on your part could stop them.

If you receive a bill and have never been afforded your administrative appeal rights, a letter under §6213(b) should be written to the Collection personnel responsible for the demand. These kinds of demands for payment are the most common, and are increasing in frequency continuously. They may be considered, for lack of a better classification, assessments arising out of mathematical or clerical errors.

Under §6213(b)(1), where the IRS discovers a mathematical or clerical error in a return, they may assess "what would have been the correct amount of tax but for the mathematical or clerical error," without regard to the deficieny procedures discussed earlier. They are very quick to make these recomputation assessments, but are extremely lax in describing your rights once such an assessment has been made. All they do is demand payment — now.

According to §6213(b)(2), within 60 days of receiving such a notice, you have the right to request an abatement of the tax, and "upon receipt of such request, the Secretary[2] shall abate the assessment. Any reassessment of the tax. . .shall be subject to the deficiency procedures" which we have described in Chapter Two.

To state these provisions more simply, when the IRS sends you a demand for tax which has been assessed before you've had an opportunity to petition the Tax Court or otherwise object to the assessment, you have the right to, within 60 days of the date of the notice and demand, request that the tax be abated. If abated, the tax will be removed from the assessment records and you will no longer owe it. **The IRS has no alternative in removing the assessment**, so long as you act within the 60-day period. Unfortunately for millions, the IRS doesn't bother to tell you that these rights exist.

Once the tax has been abated, if the IRS is convinced that you do indeed owe the additional tax, they must mail you a notice of deficiency. You will then be afforded the opportunity to contest the deficiency in Tax Court without having to first pay the tax. See Questions 67-69.

If any collection efforts are undertaken after you have mailed the §6213(b)(2) abatement letter, the IRS would be

---

[2] Referring to the Secretary of the Treasury, or his delegate, the Commissioner of IRS or his authorized agent.

proceeding illegally and could be stopped from taking any of your property or money.

QUESTION 83
Must I use any special language when objecting to an improper bill?

A case of recent vintage speaks to this very point. In **Bothke v. Fluor Engineers and Constructors, Inc.**,[3] the United States Court of Appeals for the Ninth Circuit considered a case where IRS began collection of taxes pursuant to a §6213 recomputation. The history of the case tells us that the citizen against whom the tax was assessed was notified that IRS had made a "correction to Arithmetic" and that based upon "information received," had increased his tax from zero to $6,755.80.

A notice of the kind we have just discussed was mailed and within 60 days he objected to the assessment. The key point made by the three-judge panel in this case is that although Bothke did not specifically identify his letter as complying with §6213(b)(2), "Bothke's strongly worded protest should reasonably have been construed as a request for abatement." The Court also pointed out that "The Service, however, with its expertise, is obliged to know its own governing statutes and to apply them realistically."

The case teaches us that when the objection to payment is made within the specified time, the IRS has the obligation — as they are the "experts" — to correctly construe the letter to be a request for abatement. The statute, as the court also pointed out, does not require that the letter "put a legal classification" on the protest. It merely requires that a protest be made within the 60-day period.

I have found that it is better to classify your letter if you can. But we now know from the case authority that such classifications are unnecessary.

QUESTION 84
Will they try to collect even after my letter of protest?

I have seen cases where, after the letter of protest is mailed, all collection action ceases. I have also seen cases, such as the pilot's case, and other cases similar in nature, where all letters

---
[3] 713 F.2d 1405 (9th Cir. 1983).

of protest go unheeded and the IRS barrels along oblivious to all invocation of statutory protections.

When you write a letter of protest, be prepared to back it up. If you are convinced that they are not entitled to the money, you may have to take legal action to make your view stick. Just what kind of legal action is available to you will be discussed later.

QUESTION 85
What can I do if they try to collect money which I don't owe?

Let's answer this question in two parts.

First, we'll deal with a situation where a case is pending in the Tax Court. We now know that once a petition is filed with the Tax Court within the time set by the statute[4], the IRS cannot take collection action until the Tax Court has rendered a final decision on the case. If they do, the statute says that such action "may be enjoined by a proceeding in the proper court." See §6213(a).

An injunction is an order which a court can issue that prevents a person from taking action he might otherwise take. The statute just referred to makes it possible to obtain such an order from "the proper court." The next question is, which court is the proper court? The natural tendency is for a person to complain to the Tax Court about the improper collection action. In the past, however, this course has proven futile, since the Tax Court does not have the authority to enjoin the IRS.

Therefore, the proper court would seem to be the local United States District Court for your state and district. In making application to the District Court for an injunction, you would have to demonstrate 1) that you have filed a petition with the Tax Court within the time set out in the statute, and 2) that the Tax Court has not rendered a decision in your case. Having made such a showing, you would have the right to a declaration from the district court to the effect that the IRS may not legally continue their collection action until after the Tax Court has ruled, and may then only collect what the Tax Court says is due.

---

[4] Ninety days for citizens living in the United States.

Next, let's deal with the situation where you are not in Tax Court because you've never been sent a notice of deficiency, yet the IRS has mailed a bill and is attempting to collect it. First, you must be sure that you have complied with §6213(b)(2). That is, you have mailed your letter of protest and have demanded an abatement of the tax within the 60-day period established by the statute.

Having done this, you would be entitled to file an application for injunction with the district court. If you could show that the IRS has not followed the proper administrative procedures in making their assessment, you would be entitled to the injunction. We have summarized what constitutes the proper administrative procedures leading to assessment. To review, you must be given a notice of deficiency and the IRS must wait until the Tax Court has ruled. If a recomp letter is mailed and you object within 60 days, they must abate the tax.

One profound teaching of the **Bothke** case is that the IRS will not be allowed to carry out collection action where they have not complied with their own administrative procedures in making assessments.

QUESTION 86
Are there any circumstances in which a tax may be assessed without regard to the deficiency procedures?

Two circumstances come to mind. One we have already mentioned in Question 46, involving certain penalties which may be assessed without regard to the deficiency procedures established by the Code. These penalties come under Chapter 68 of the Code, and encompass several areas. The penalties run from §§6671 through 6704 and the most common apply to failure to file certain information returns, such as W-2s or 1099s, for which there is a penalty. The penalty may be assessed and collected without regard to the deficiency procedures. Two of the more common such penalties fall under §§6682 and 6702.

Section 6682 creates a penalty of $500 for filing a withholding statement with one's employer[5] which 1) results in a reduction of the amount of withholding of federal income tax on his wages, and 2) at the time the statement was made there was no reasonable basis for the statement.

---
[5] A withholding statement is a Form W-4 which is filed with your employer at the time you begin work. The form is created under §3402 of the Code.

116 YOUR WORST FEARS

Section 6702 creates a penalty of $500 for filing an income tax return which 1) does not contain information from which the correctness of the computation of tax can be determined, or 2) which contains information that on its face indicates that the computation of tax is incorrect.

The so-called assessable penalties are numerous, and relate to many different circumstances. We have here covered just two examples. In each case, since the tax is assessed and collected without regard to the deficiency procedures, you always have a right to claim a refund of the penalty once it is collected.

In some cases, the particular statute creating the penalty also establishes rules governing the refund of these penalties. For example, §6703 sets out specific steps which must be taken in order to contest the penalties under §§6700, 6701 and 6702.[6]

When faced with the imposition of these penalties, the rules should be read carefully so that you can protect all of your rights if you care to contest the penalty by demanding a refund of it.

The second condition under which the IRS may assess a tax without regard to deficiency procedures is the so-called jeopardy assessment. The jeopardy assessment is a most formidable collection tool and finds its origin in §6861 of the Code. That section permits the IRS to immediately assess and collect the tax if it "believes" that assessment or collection would be "jeopardized by delay."

While the IRS may make an assessment and begin collection of taxes without prior notice under §6861, certain procedures must be followed both before and after the assessment is made.

First, there must be a finding that one of these three conditions exists: a) the citizen is leaving or planning to leave the country; b) the citizen is or is planning to defeat the payment of his taxes by concealing, transferring or dissipating his property; or c) his financial solvency is imperiled.

After it is determined that one of these conditions exists, the district director must personally review the jeopardy assessment. In the process, the assessment will also be reviewed by district counsel, the IRS lawyers, but their review

---

[6] We have already discussed §6702. Sections 6700 and 6701 establish penalties for tax shelter promoters and tax return perparers.

is not for procedural purposes. They look at it to determine whether it will be defendable if the citizen objects to it later.

Once the approval of the district director is given, the assessment is immediately made. The citizen is then served with a) a Notice of Jeopardy Assessment, which will include the examining agent's notes and computations, b) a demand for immediate payment of the tax, and c) a form letter explaining the appeal rights with regard to the jeopardy assessment.

Having followed these administrative procedures, a jeopardy assessment will be immediately collectable by the IRS through enforced collection action.

QUESTION 87
Are there limitations which apply to jeopardy assessments?

The Code places restrictions on the IRS after a jeopardy assessment is made. The first such restriction is that within 60 days of the date the assessment is made, a notice of deficiency must be sent to the citizen, giving him an opportunity to contest the assessment in the Tax Court. See §6861(b). As always, you have the option of paying the amount assessed and filing a claim for refund within the time set by law. This procedure has been discussed earlier.

A jeopardy assessment may be made where a petition with the Tax Court has already been filed. For example, suppose the IRS has mailed a notice of deficiency to you and, within the 90-day grace period, you file a petition with the Tax Court. If, after the petition is filed, the IRS believes that collection of the tax is in jeopardy, they can make a jeopardy assessment even though the case is already in the Tax Court. If this is done, the Tax Court has the authority to adjust the assessment upward or downward, depending upon the outcome of the case. See §6861(c).

If the jeopardy assessment is made after the Tax Court decision has been rendered, then the amount of the assessment is limited by the amount the Tax Court has determined as the deficiency. See §6861(d). After the Tax Court's decision has become final, or the citizen has filed an appeal of the Tax Court's decision, the IRS has lost its right to make a jeopardy assessment. See §6861(e).

Another important restriction upon the jeopardy assessment comes into play when the IRS has seized property pursuant to the assessment. The property may not be sold until the decision of the Tax Court has become final, or, if no petition is filed, until the 90-day grace period for doing so has passed. See §6863(b).

So, while you may be deprived of the use of your property in a jeopardy assessment situation, it cannot be sold until there is a decision from the Tax Court on your case, unless you waive your rights by not petitioning the Court within the time period.

QUESTION 88
Are jeopardy assessments appealable?

As you can imagine, a jeopardy assessment, and the immediate collection of tax which accompanies it, can be very devastating. Even though you have the right to petition the Tax Court to have the assessment redetermined, in the meantime all of your assets are subject to seizure by the IRS. It is true that property seized cannot generally be sold, but you are nevertheless deprived of the use of it until the assessment question can be cleared up.

In the meantime, Congress has, in the Tax Reform Act of 1976, provided two means of immediately calling into question the propriety of the assessment. The first way, under §7429, is to make an administrative appeal asking that the assessment be reviewed. Under the law, within 5 days of making the jeopardy assessment, the IRS must provide the citizen with a written statement setting out the information upon which the assessment is based. You would then have 30 days in which to file a request that the assessment be reviewed to determine its propriety.

Where such a request is made, the IRS will consider 1) whether it was "reasonable" to make the jeopardy assessment and 2) whether the amount assessed is "appropriate" under the circumstances. After review of all the facts and circumstances, including the material provided in a post-assessment conference, the IRS can abate its jeopardy assessment "in whole or in part."

The conference is held before the Appeals Office, and an expeditious hearing is called for. A conference will be held and a decision made within sixteen days of the date the request for an administrative appeal was made.

At the hearing, consideration will be given to the appropriateness of making a jeopardy assessment. As we learned in the previous question, such an assessment can only be made where the IRS has found that 1) you are preparing to leaving the country, 2) you have designs to dissipate your assets so as to evade payment of the tax, or 3) your solvency is imperiled.

All of your efforts to have the assessment abated, therefore, must focus upon those three factual areas. You will have to be prepared to present such evidence as will convince the Appeals Officer that none of the three conditions exist, and that the assessment is therefore erroneous.

You may also challenge the amount of the assessment at the conference. Any and all data which you believe will aid the development of an accurate picture of your financial condition will help.

If the assessment is sustained in whole or in part by the Appeals Office, the stage is set for the next level of appeal, the judicial review. Under §7429(b), you may file an application with the district court for an expedited review of the assessment.

In the action, the court will determine two questions. The first is whether making the jeopardy assessment was "reasonable under all the circumstances" and 2) whether the amount assessed "is appropriate under the circumstances." See §7429(b)(2). In making these decisions, the court will look at all facts and circumstances which have a bearing on the case.

The time for filing an application for judicial review under §7429 is, as you should know by now, fixed and must be strictly adhered to. A petition for judicial review can be filed within 30 days of the earlier of a) the day the IRS renders its decision on the administrative appeal, or b) sixteen days from the date on which the request for administrative review was made. The petition would be filed with your local United States district court.

Once the action is filed, the court has 20 days in which to make a decision, and this period can only be extended if the citizen agrees to such an extension. The decision of the court is final and cannot be appealed. See §7429(f).

In the hearing, the IRS must prove the appropriateness of making the assessment (remember the three criteria?) and you would have the burden to prove that the amount of the assessment is improper. See §7429(g).

QUESTION 89
Can I sue the IRS?

In most circumstances, the IRS cannot be sued. The Anti-Injunction Act, §7421 of Code, does not allow the courts to hear suits "with respect to the assessment or collection of taxes." This Act, more than any other single factor, has enabled the IRS to run roughshod over the rights of the citizens of this country. IRS is of a mind that they can do anything they want in the collection of taxes, and, because of the Act, nobody can do anything about it.

The Fifth Amendment to the Constitution provides in part that a person cannot be deprived of life, liberty or property without due process of law. Due process has been defined as requiring a notice and opportunity to be heard before any deprivation of those assets occurs. Where the IRS is concerned, these rights are greatly curtailed by the Act.

The courts, in an effort to militate an illegitmate condition, have said that the government's interest in the speedy collection of its revenue outweighs the individual's right to due process of law. Due process is in fact afforded a citizen, the courts say, because he has the right to sue the government for a refund of any taxes which have been improperly collected.

What the courts are in essence saying is that you, the average citizen, are in a better position to withstand the improper deprivation of your property — say $2,000 in tax money — than is the United States Government. For that reason, your rights must wither when pitted against their's.

The Anti-Injunction Act notwithstanding, the Congress and the courts have carved out exceptions to the Act which, when used creatively, can bypass the apparent resolute nature of the Act's provisions. These exceptions have been used successfully in recent litigation to hold the IRS at bay in cases where they have clearly overstepped their bounds, even when measured against the broad yardstick of their own regulations.

The first exception is a Congressionally created right which comes into play should the IRS attempt to seize the property of a person who has no tax liability. Section 7426 creates the so-called "wrongful levy" action. It applies where the collection tools available to the IRS have been used against persons who have no unpaid tax liability, or where the proper administrative procedures have not been followed.

Because of the IRS' quite common "shotgun" approach to the collection of taxes, it is not unusual for them to levy property belonging to a person other than the citizen whose liability is being forceably collected. Under these circumstances, where the property being seized belongs to a person who does not owe any taxes, a suit may be filed by that person to enjoin the seizure or sale of that property.

The second exception, which we have already discussed, arises where the tax liability was not assessed in accordance with the proper administrative procedures set forth in the Code. The case of **Bothke v. Fluor Engineers** and Constructors[7] allows even the "taxpayer" — the person against whom the tax was assessed — to file a suit to enjoin collection when he has been deprived of his administrative rights in connection with making the assessment.

Bothke, you will recall, was sent a notice that his liability had been recomputed by the Service Center in accordance with §6213. Bothke responded with a request to have the assessment abated within the prescribed 60-day period, but the IRS ignored his request. They went forward to collect the tax and he sued.

The court found that his lawsuit was a proper undertaking, §7421 notwithstanding, since the IRS had not followed the requisite administrative procedures in making the assessment in the first place. As the 9th Circuit pointed out:

> "Merely demanding payment, even repeatedly, does not cause liability.*** The Service may assess the tax only in certain circumstances and in conformity with proper procedures." 713 F.2d at 1414.

Where they have failed to do so, the collection of the tax may be enjoined.

The third exception to the Act grows out of decades of litigation with the IRS over the collection of taxes. The Anti-Injunction Act is not a new face in the crowd of tax statutes. It has been around, in one form or another, since the late 1800's, when the United States first got serious about the collection of revenue.

---

[7] See note 3.

122 YOUR WORST FEARS

A series of Supreme Court cases dating back to nearly the birth of the Act have created a condition where the "taxpayer" may enjoin collection of the tax if he can show the existence of certain conditions. The latest case in the series, which relies a great deal upon two earlier cases, is **Commissioner v. Shapiro**.[8]

Under the **Shapiro** doctrine, an injunction against collection will be issued if the applicant can show: 1) that under no circumstances can the government sustain its claim that taxes are due, based upon all of the facts available at the time of the suit, 2) that the citizen will suffer irreparable harm[9] if collection of the tax is carried out, and 3) that he has no adequate alternative means of preventing the damage which will be occasioned by enforced collection.

The first prong of the test relates to the liability itself. Where it is shown that the assessment is arbitrary, excessive and without foundation, you are no longer dealing with the collection of taxes, but merely "exactions in the guise of a tax."[10] If the IRS cannot support its assessment with facts sufficient to create the substantial likelihood that you in fact owe the tax assessed, then the court would be entitled to hold that the first prong has been met.

The second prong relates to your ability to financially withstand the collection action. If it can be demonstrated that you will suffer irreparable harm — financial constraints which will result in irreversable hardship — then you have met the second requirement of the test.

Lastly, you must prove that the administrative avenues available are not adequate to prevent your sustaining the kind of hardship which could be classified as "irreparable harm." This showing must come on the heels of proving that the assessment is arbitrary and excessive in the first place.

The third point is the one which poses the most difficulty in injunction actions. The government is always quick to point out that the "taxpayer has the remedy of paying the tax and suing for a refund." This remedy, they maintain, will prevent any enforced collection action and provides protection from the financial ruin you claim will arise. You must be prepared to

---

[8] 424 U.S. 614 (1976).
[9] This referes to the kind of damage or injury which cannot be repared by money or money's worth.
[10] See **Miller v. Standard Nut Margarine Co.**, 248 U.S. 498 (1932), the first of the key Supreme Court cases mentioned earlier. See also **Enochs v. Williams Packing Co.**, 370 U.S. 1 (1962).

show why the payment remedy is inadequate, and will itself lead to crushing financial constraints.

Only when all three tests are met will the court grant an injunction preventing the IRS from collecting the tax. While the test is difficult to meet, it is not impossible. What is equally important in these cases is dealing with the position universally taken by government attorneys that the Anti-Injunction Act forbids **all** suits against the IRS, regardless of the circumstances.

Government attorneys do no like to admit that exceptions to this rule exist, and the courts are quick to side with them in these debates. If you find yourself in this kind of battle, you'll do well to understand the lawful sweep of the Anti-Injunction Act, and, more importantly, its limitations. It very well could be the difference between success or failure in a suit against the IRS.

QUESTION 90
What can the IRS do to "enforce collection" of taxes?

Before enforced collection can be undertaken, the IRS must have a valid assessment, lawfully obtained through the administrative process. They must then make demand on the taxpayer for payment. No enforced collection action can be taken until 10 days after the demand has been made. See §6331. After demand has been made and no payment is forthcoming, the amount of the tax, interest and penalty becomes a lien in favor of the United States against "all property and rights to property, whether real or personal," belonging to the debtor. See §6321.

Section 6331 permits levy upon all "property and rights to property" once the 10-day period has expired and the tax hasn't been paid. The act of levying involves the taking of one's personal assets to satisfy the unpaid liability. "All" assets include bank accounts, stocks, bonds, personal property of value such as jewelry, coin or gun collections, or any other property in which the debtor has an interest. Real property includes houses, buildings, land or any other property of a real character in which you may have an interest.

With regard to real property, there are two ways in which the levy can be carried out. The first is the administrative process, which involves seizing the property under the authority of §6331. The property is then sold and the proceeds are applied first to the costs of the sale, and then to the tax bill.

The second method is for the Department of Justice, on behalf of the United States, to commence an action to reduce the assessment to judgment, and to have the judgment executed against a parcel of property. This procedure grows out of §7403 of the Code, and is generally followed where other persons not in debt with the IRS claim an interest in the property. The court, under §7403, has the power to declare the nature and extent of the interest of the other parties, and provide that those interests be protected, either by preventing sale of the property, or by ordering just compensation if sale is permitted.[11]

The IRS can also levy upon wages and salaries, on a continuing basis, to satisfy the tax, and can seize tax refunds to which you are entitled for other years.

QUESTION 91
How much of my paycheck can be seized?

The levy upon wages and salaries is one of the most, if not the most, offensive powers which the IRS has. The reason is because there is no percentage limit on the amount of money they can take. When under levy, you are given what amounts to an allowance for those persons whose support you pay. No consideration whatsoever is made for other financial commitments, such as bank loans, or other fixed payments.

If you are single and only support yourself, you are allowed one "exemption" from the levy, which is worth just $75. Thus, if you earn $500 per week, in addition to the normal tax withholding taken from your check, the IRS will seize everything else, leaving you with but $75 upon which to live for the week.

For each additional person whose support you are responsible to pay, you will be entitled to another $25 exemption. This will include your spouse. So if you are married and have two children, you will be entitled to keep $150 of your weekly wages or salary upon which to live. These amounts are provided for in §6334 of the Code.

---

[11] **United States v. Rogers**, 461 U.S. 677 (1983).

QUESTION 92
Can my homestead be seized?

Homestead laws are state created protections for debtors. The federal law, and not the state law, determines what property can be seized and sold for federal tax obligations. The federal law creates no exemption for homestead property. As a result, homestead property, to the extent that it is a property right, can be seized and sold for federal tax bills.[12]

The important factor to consider here is this: While the federal law determines what property can be sold, state law determines what constitutes ownership of property, or, under what conditions property rights are said to exist. If, for some reason under state law, you do not have a "right" in the property which the IRS intends to seize, that property cannot be taken to satisfy your tax debt.[13]

QUESTION 93
If I own property jointly with my spouse, can it still be seized?

This area has been the subject of much litigation over the years, and recently the Supreme Court has put the question to rest. In **United States v. Rogers**,[14] the Supreme Court considered the question of whether homestead property held jointly by a husband and wife could be sold where **only** the husband had an unpaid tax liability. Contrary to the ruling of the lower courts, the Supreme Court held that the property could be sold, but that the separate property rights of the non-debtor spouse had to be compensated.

In that case, the government argued that the statute under which judicial sale is generally sought — §7403 — mandates sale of the property. From the standpoint of the citizen, the Supreme Court did shed favorable light upon the judicial sale question. They held that the statute did not "require" sale of the property, but rather pointed out that the district court had the power to prevent sale where the interests of the non-debtor spouse could not be adequately compensated with money. As the Supreme Court said in the case, "money is not always adequate compensation for a roof over one's head."

---

[12] See **Rogers**, note 11.
[13] **Aquilino v. United States**, 363 U.S. 509 (1960).
[14] See note 11.

126 YOUR WORST FEARS

Where it can be shown that the non-debtor spouse will be irreparably harmed through the sale, and that money's worth compensation will be inadequate to rectify this damage, sale of the homestead should not be ordered.

It must be pointed out that where a spouse signs a joint income tax return, or the assessment is in her name as well as the husband's, even though she may not have had separate income, the liability will be the responsibility of both. The IRS can collect the tax by levy upon property belonging to either or both of them. If no joint return is in question, though, the IRS will have to compensate the non-debtor spouse for her interest in the property.

QUESTION 94
If my spouse signed a joint return but didn't have income, can she be made to pay the tax?

Ordinarily, in signing a joint return, both parties accept full responsibility for the tax shown on the return. Even though one of those parties may not have been the principal income earner, he or she will nevertheless be held accountable for payment of the tax.

There is a provision of law, however, which affords relief to the so-called "innocent spouse" where certain tests are met. Section 6013(e) is the innocent spouse statute, and it has three elements. First, a joint return must have been filed which omits 25% of the gross income. Second, the spouse must have no knowledge of the omission. And last, the spouse must not have benefitted from the omission.

As to the first element, if a spouse files her own return, or files no return at all, the benefits of §6013(e) will not apply. A joint return must be the source of the liability. This is because a joint return ordinarily makes both signers "jointly" liabile for the tax. If a spouse files her own return, she cannot be held liable for the husband's liability.

Secondly, the "knowledge" aspect of the test is crucial in determining entitlement to the innocent spouse statute. Where a spouse had actual knowledge of the omissions, she will not be afforded the protections of the statute. However, for "joint" liability to attach to her, it is not necessary that she had "actual" knowledge. If she had reason to know by virtue of participation in the family finances, or was cognizant of large deposits or lavish or unusual expenditures, the court may well hold that the spouse had "knowledge" of the understatement thereby depriving her of innocent spouse protections.

The last element is the "benefit" element. If the spouse can show that she did not benefit from the omission, even where the other two elements are shown, the court will not hold her liable for payment of the tax. Tax regulations state that normal support does not constitute "significant benefit" depriving her of innocent spouse status.[15]

However, transfers of property to the spouse, and lavish or unusual expenditures in her favor will be taken into consideration in the "benefit" test. The court will also consider such intangibles as whether the innocent spouse has been deserted by or divorced from the guilty spouse. These intangibles will be weighed in considering whether it is "equitable" — or fair — to hold the innocent spouse liable for the debt.

QUESTION 95
Can I avoid seizure of my property by just giving it away?

Where property has been transferred, or given to another, such an exchange may give rise to a "transferee liability." Under the rules of transferee liability, the IRS may void a transfer if it is found to meet several criteria.

Under an extension of a rule established through the English Common Law, where a transfer of property is accomplished strictly to defraud creditors of a means of satisfying a judgment, then that transfer will said to be void. This, in essence, is what a transferee liability is.

Several states have enacted similar provisions, and a uniform body of statutes, not unlike the Uniform Commerical Code, has been enacted. This body of law, called the Uniform Fraudulent Conveyances Act, enables a given creditor to void a transfer of property where it can be shown that the transfer affected the creditor's right to collect a judgment.

There as several elements to a fraudulent transfer. They are that:
1) property was transferred from the debtor to a third party;
2) the debtor was liable for a tax;
3) the tax is still unpaid;

---
[15] See Rev. Reg. §1.6013-5(b).

4) the transfer was made at the time the tax liability existed;

5) the transfer was made without full or adequate consideration;

6) the transfer left the debtor insolvent; and

7) the government has exhausted all other means of collecting the debt against the debtor before proceeding against the third party.

The first three elements of this showing are rather self-explanatory, so let's begin our discussion with the fourth element.

To prove the existence of the fourth element, the liability need not have been **assessed** against the citizen at the time of the transfer; it need only have **accrued**. That is, where the tax liability grows out of income earned during a particular year, but not assessed until one year later, the tax will be said to have accrued in the year in which the income was earned. With this rule in mind, a transfer of property cannot be said to be fraudulent when the tax in question is on income earned in a year subsequent to the property transfer.

Suppose, for example, you transfer your house to a third party in 1984. In 1985 year earn income and in 1986, an assessment is made based upon that income. The transfer in 1984 cannot be fraudulent because the liability did not accrue until 1985, the year the income was earned. On the other hand, if the property was transferred in late 1985, and the tax was not assessed until mid 1986, that transfer could be said to fraudulent, since the liability accrued in 1985, the year the income was earned.

The fifth element holds that the property must have been transferred without full or adequate consideration. The term "consideration" grows out of contract law and relates to full or adequate payment in exchange for goods or services, making the exchange one of equal value. When one agrees to transfer a parcel of property valued at $50,000 in exchange for money or money's worth equal to $50,000, then the transfer was for full and adequate consideration.

Conversely, where the same parcel is transferred as a gift, or for something less than $50,000 in money or money's worth, than it could be argued that the transfer wasn't for full and adequate consideration.

The sixth element is that the transfer must leave the debtor insolvent. The mere act of transferring property to a third party does not bring into play the Uniform Fraudulent Conveyances Act. It comes into play only when creditors are deprived of an opportunity to satisfy their judgment against the debtor. Where the transfer leaves the debtor without any other property against which the judgment can be executed, a fraudulent conveyance may come into existence if all other elements are met.

The seventh and last element is that the government has exhausted all other means of satisfying their judgment against the debtor. For example, if the government has an avenue of pursuit available against the debtor which it has not yet pursued, then they will be foreclosed from pursuing third parties to whom property was transferred until those avenues have been exhausted.

In a transferee liability case, the government must prove each and every one of the seven elements just discussed. As in every case where multiple elements must be shown, if they fail to prove any one element, their entire case will collapse. Suppose, then, that it is alleged that a transfer of property to a third party was fraudulent. Suppose further that in subsequent litigation, the government is able to prove all but the fifth element of the test. (You'll recall that the fifth element was that the transfer was made without full or adequate consideration.) Even though each of the other elements has been proven, the case against the third party will fail because the fifth element is missing.

Based upon the law of fraudulent conveyances, we can say that simply "giving property away" will not necessarily prevent its being seized and sold. If the government can prove that the seven elements of a fraudulent conveyance exist, the transfer can be voided and the property seized. Of course, if a fraudulent conveyance could not be proved, the government would be powerless to, in any way, affect the transfer.

QUESTION 96
What property is exempt from seizure?

The Code has a provision for exempting property from seizure. We have discussed it briefly in Question 91. Section 6334 is the only authority given by Congress for exempting property from levy. We find that no specific class of property is totally exempt — only minimum amounts of certain classes. What this means is that any and all property which the debtor owns or has a right to can be levied upon to pay the tax. But, certain amounts of such property have been set aside as exempt.

The statute allows nine such exemptions. They are:

1. Clothing and school books of the debtor and his family;
2. Fuel, provisions, furniture, and personal effects, the value of which does not exceed $1,500;
3. Books and tools of one's trade or business not exceeding $1,000 in value;
4. Unemployment benefits;
5. Undelivered mail;
6. Annuity and pension payments under the Railroad Retirement Act, benefits under the Railroad Unemployment Insurance Act, and certain other pension payments related to armed forces personnel;
7. Workmen's compensation payments;
8. Judgments for the support of minor children; and
9. Minimum exemptions for wages, salary, and other income. The exemption amounts to $75 per week for the debtor, plus $25 additional for his spouse and each minor child.

As you can see, there isn't very much which the IRS can't levy upon in order to satisfy an unpaid tax bill.

QUESTION 97
Can my pension or Social Security payments be levied?

Unless your pension falls into category 6 of the previous question, the answer is yes. However, the IRS has established some guidelines with regard to Social Security and pension payments.

The IRS Manual for revenue officers points out[16] that Social Security payments, qualified pension plans, benefits under the G.I. Bill of Rights, self-employed pension plans (Keogh), and IRAs, are subject to levy. It stipulates, however, that levy of these pensions could defeat the purpose of the laws creating the plans in the first place, and could cause hardships to the persons against whom the levy is executed.

Therefore, the Manual says, levy of these sources of "income" should be made "only in flagrant and aggravated cases, and then only with the prior approval of the authorized service employee who will sign the notice of levy."

---
[16] See IRM Part V, Collection 5331.1, MT 5-261 (June 4, 1984).

The Manual goes on to point out that it is difficult to "establish criteria" for determining which cases are "flagrant and aggravated," but gives some suggestions. They are:
1. The amount of the liability;
2. The amount which may be obtained through service of a single notice of levy;
3. The possibility of collection from other sources; and
4. Whether the debtor is relying upon this source of income as his chief means of support, and whether deprivation of it would cause hardship.

Any levy of income from these sources must be approved by the Chief of the Collection Field carrying out the levy, or the district director if there is no Chief.

QUESTION 98
How long does the IRS have to collect a tax?

Once a tax has been assessed, unless you would agree to an extension that tax must be collected within six years of the date of the assessment. The six-year time period is extended only if: 1) you, the debtor agree to extend it, or 2) the IRS commences an action in court with respect to collection within the six year period. See §6503.

Once court action is commenced, such as a §7403 action, the statute is tolled and they may continue collection action until the tax is paid. However, the execution of a single wage levy, a purely administrative act, is not a **court action** with respect to collection, and this kind of administrative collection activity is not enough to extend the period of limitations. Moreover, once judicial collection action is taken, the IRS may not then resort to administrative collection. All collection activity must remain judicial in nature.

QUESTION 99
How long does a tax lien last?

The duration or life of a general tax lien is tied directly to the statute of limitations on collections. Thus, the life of the lien is six years, unless an action in court is commenced within that period of time. See §6322. If judicial collection action is taken, then the lien will continue in effect, and will remain superior to that of other creditors until the tax is paid.

QUESTION 100
Are there any limitations on the manner in which the IRS may execute its levy?

The main limitation which you should be aware of is the six-year rule. Under §6503, the IRS has six years in which to collect the taxes, or bring a proceeding in court to do so. Once the six years have lapsed, they are not free to make an administrative levy upon any property. Indeed, if they have not commenced an action in court by that time, they are prohibited from taking any further collection action. Under §6322, the general tax lien would then expire.

Once any action in court has been commenced, after the expiration of the six-year period the only way in which further collection can be carried out is under court supervision. Let me illustrate. Suppose a tax liability is assessed on January 1, 1984. The IRS would have until January 1, 1990, in which to satisfy its assessment administratively. Suppose further, that on June 1, 1988, they levy upon a bank account and collect one half the assessment, but take no further action to collect. Come January 1, 1990, they will have to be happy with only half the tax due, because that's all they can legally collect.

Now, assuming the same facts, let's suppose that after the administrative levy is carried out, but before the six-year period expires, the IRS commences a suit in court to have their general lien declared a personal judgment against the debtor. With the commencement of that action, the IRS is free to collect the assessment beyond the six-year period, but can only do so under court supervision growing out of the suit.

Levy authority is also limited in a Constitutional sense. The IRS is not free to violate Fourth Amendment privacy rights in the collection of taxes through administrative levy. In the case of **G.M. Leasing Corp. v. United States**[17] revenue officers effected forced entry to the premises of a corporation's offices. While there, they seized the books and records of the corporation, along with other property. The court found the seizure of the material to be invalid because the revenue officers did not have a warrant permitting entry to and search of the private property.

Where seizure of property is done in violation of the Fourth Amendment, the victim of the unlawful action has several remedies available. The first is the return of the seized

---

[17] 429 U.S. 338 (1977).

property, including photocopies of any documents taken, suppression of any evidence obtained as a result of the illegal seizure, and general and punitive damages against the revenue officers who have acted illegally.[18]

QUESTION 101
Can I be made to pay the tax debts of a corporation?

Section 6672 of the Code establishes the so-called 100 percent penalty. The penalty applies in the case of individuals who: 1) were required "to collect, truthfully account for and pay over" employment taxes, and 2) who willfully failed to do so. The penalty attaches to individual directors and officers of corporations and is "equal to" the tax which was to have been paid over, but which was not. Hence the appellation "100 percent penalty."

The penalty is assessed against those "persons responsible" for carrying out the duties incident to the payment of the taxes. Whether a person was in a position to do so is a question of fact and is decided on the basis of all the circumstances of the case. Some factors which the courts will look to in determining whether a given person is "responsible" for the payment of the tax, and concomitantly, the 100 percent penalty, are:

1. Who had the power to decide what creditors were to be paid and how much they were to be paid? The signing or co-signing of corporation checks is often viewed as indicative of such responsibility.[19]

2. Who prepared or signed payroll tax returns in the past, or for the periods in which the tax went unpaid? The courts may well assume that the person preparing the returns was also responsible to see that the taxes were paid.[20]

3. What do the corporate bylaws say about the responsibilities of the various corporate officers? The corporate officer charged in the bylaws with a duty to carry out the obligations incident to federal payroll tax laws will not fare well where the 100 percent penalty is concerned.[21]

4. Who are the officers, directors, or principal shareholders of the corporation? Some courts have said that these persons

---

[18] See **G.M. Leasing Corp**, note 17.
[19] **Cash v. Campbell**, 346 F.2d 670 (5th Cir. 1965).
[20] **Horowitz v. United States**, 339 F.2d 877 (2nd Cir. 1965).
[21] **United States v. Streble**, 313 F.2d 402 (8th Cir. 1963).

are presumed responsible for the tax, but where evidence to the contrary is presented, that presumption can be dissolved.[22]

5. Who directed the payment of other creditors rather than the United States? This person may be held accountable for the payment of the 100 percent penalty.[23]

The second element of the 100 percent penalty is very important and can mean the difference between whether or not the penalty will be assessed as to a particular person. The element, that of "willfulness," must be shown in addition to any of the above factors before a person can be forced to pay the penalty. Willfulness, as we have seen earlier,[24] is the voluntary, intentional violation of a known legal duty. It is distinguished from mistake, negligence, or some other action which could be characterized as less than deliberate conduct.[25]

Thus, were it can be shown that you did not act "willfully" in connection with failure to pay the tax, either by reason of ignorance, or some other non-willful reason, the tax should not be assessed against you.[26]

QUESTION 102
How do I contest the 100 percent penalty?

The 100 percent penalty is an assessable penalty. As you will recall from our discussion of assessable penalties (Question 86), the IRS need not adhere to the deficiency rules when making the assessment. Thus, when the 100 percent penalty is asserted and becomes assessed, the IRS will send a notice and demand that it be paid. Since the Tax Court does not have jurisdiction over employment tax disputes,[27] the only available remedy is to pay the tax and file a claim for refund, followed by a suit for refund if the claim is denied.

Ordinarily, the entire amount of tax must be paid when the refund procedures are contemplated. This is not true with employment taxes. The employment tax is a "devisable" tax. It can be separated into smaller amounts based upon quarters of a year. To illustrate, consider the hypothetical case where the IRS has assessed one amount of $20,000 as the 100 percent penalty for two years, or eight calendar quarters. Now

---

[22] **McCarty v. United States**, 437 F.2d 961 (Ct. Cl. 1971).
[23] See **Horowitz**, note 20.
[24] See Questions 39 and 114.
[25] See **United States v. Pomponio**, 429 U.S. 10 (1976), and **Kalb v. United States**, 505 F.2d 506 (2nd Cir. 1974.
[26] **United States v. Leuschner**, 336 F.2d 246 (9th Cir. 1964).
[27] See §§6212(a) and 6213(a).

suppose that the smallest amount for any one quarter was $1,500. The single amount of $1,500 can be paid and such payment will be sufficient to commence the refund process.[28]

QUESTION 103
If my property is held in trust, can it be seized?

A trust is created where one person gives property to another, to be held for the benefit of a third. For example, if I give my wife $10 and instruct her to give it to my brother when she sees him, a trust is created. I would be considered the creator of the trust, my wife the trustee, and my brother the beneficiary.

If I tell her to give the money back to me if she doesn't see him within a stated period of time, I have created a revocable trust. If I tell her that she is to give him the money, and under no circumstances, is she to return it to me, I have created an irrevocable trust.

Ordinarily, property held in trust is not subject to seizure for payment of the tax liability of the creator. This general rule can be set aside however, where it is shown that the trust was created as a ruse to avoid taxes, i.e., the conveyance of property in trust was a fraudulent conveyance. Also, when the creator of the trust continues to exercise power and dominion over the assets of the trust, the trust assets will be considered his assets for tax collection purposes.

In order that a trust avoid being "pierced" for tax collection purposes, it will have to be shown that the creator of the trust does not exercise any power or dominion over the disposition of the assets of the trust. Also, the conditions of the Uniform Fraudulent Conveyances Act must not be present in the transaction. See Question 95.

QUESTION 104
What rules must be followed when the IRS sells seized property?

Both before and during the sale of seized property, the IRS must follow clearly defined procedures. These procedures are set out in §6335 of the Code.

Before the sale, the IRS must provide a notice of seizure to the original owner of the property. The notice must be in writing and must be given as "soon as practicable." The

---
[28] **Flora v. United States**, 362 U.S. 145 (1960).

notice must be delivered in person, or left at the place of business or abode of the person whose property was seized. If he cannot be found, it must be mailed to his last known address. The notice must also contain the amount of tax demanded, and a description of the property which has been seized.

Next, a notice of sale must be given to the owner and must be made public. The notice of sale must also specifically describe the property to be sold, and the time, date, location and conditions of the sale. The notice must appear in a newspaper either published or circulated in the county in which the seizure was made.

Lastly, the sale cannot take place less than 10 or more than 40 days after the date of the notice of sale. Any sale which fails to follow these set procedures could be declared void.[29]

With regard to the actual sale of seized property, Code §6335 makes several stipulations. First of all, the property must be sold in the manner which is likely to bring the highest price. Before the sale, a minimum price must be set by the district office, and if the property does not sell at this minimum price, it must be declared purchased by the government at that price, and that amount, less the costs of the sale, must then be credited to the account of the debtor.[30]

The minimum price is determined on the basis of several factors, and the Internal Revenue Manual sets out standards which must be met in determining the price. These factors include wholesale prices of the item, its age and condition, its value as determined by appraisers, and any other means which would be used by a prudent businessman to determine its value.[31]

The regulations[32] command revenue officers conducting any sale to instruct perspective buyers that the property is sold "as is" and that the United States makes no warranties as to the property at all. The sale is limited to that of the rights held by the debtor. If it is determined after the sale that the debtor had no right, title or interest in the property, the purchaser has no recourse against the United States. In fact, the government will not even make any guarantees that the property actually

---

[29] **Marigotta v. District Director**, 214 F.2d 518 (2nd Cir. 1954).
[30] See Code §6343(b).
[31] IRM 5344(1)(C), MT 5-261 (June 4, 1984).
[32] Rev. Reg. §301.6335-1(c)(4)(iii).

belonged to the person from whom it was taken, making the purchase of property seized by IRS more than just a little risky.

Sales are conducted by public auction or sealed bid. See Code §6335(e)(2). If the total bid is $200 or less, the entire amount must be received by the revenue officer with the bid. If it is greater than $200, 20 percent of the bid, or $200, which ever is greater, must accompany the bid.

If nobody bids the minimum price on the property, which isn't announced until after the sale, the United States will be declared the purchaser and the bid deposits will be returned. Possession of the sale property will not be turned over to the successful bidder, if any there be, until the full price of the bid has been paid, but responsibility for the loss and storage of the property shifts to the purchaser. Thus, even though the bidder may not be able to take possession of the property, he will bear all of the expenses in connection with it, commencing with the date his bid is accepted.[33]

At the conclusion of the sale, a certificate is supposed to be given the successful bidder, which evidences the fact of the sale and the fact of the purchase. At the end of the redemption period, the certificate is supposed to be exchanged for a deed to the property (where the property is real estate), which, in turn, is supposed to operate as a transfer of all right, title and interest of the debtor to the purchaser.[34]

I say "supposed to" because I know of at least one case where property was purchased at public auction by an individual who then could not get any form of title. He was given a bill of sale but no deed. When he attempted to record his bill of sale in the county where the property was located, he was told by the Registrar's office that the bill of sale was not sufficient to enable him to have the property retitled to his name. He was then told by the Registrar that in order to have the property retitled, he would need the consent of the person from whom the property was seized. That person refused.

After confronting the government authorities with the problem, he was told, in so many words "tough luck — that's your problem." He ended up suing the government for his money back.

---

[33] Rev. Reg. §301.6335-1(c)(7).
[34] See Code §§6338 and 6339.

Records of the sale are supposed to be kept by the district director, and since the sales are public sales, a case could be made that the records of the bidders are also public. But only records of real estate sales are required to be kept.

The final requirement relates to the manner in which the proceeds of the sale are to be applied. Code §6342 establishes the following order for application of proceeds:

1. Expenses of the levy and sale;
2. Any tax on the specific item seized (this would apply in such cases as alcohol or tobacco);
3. The liability of the debtor which gave rise to the levy in the first place.

Any surplus proceeds must be either credited or refunded to the person whose property was sold.

QUESTION 105
Can I redeem seized property?

Either before or after the sale of seized property, it can be redeemed.

To redeem before the property is sold, the amount of the tax must be paid, together with the costs of levy and the costs of the anticipated sale. See Code §6337. Redemption cannot be accomplished by paying merely the value of the seized property. The entire tax must be paid.

After the sale, personal property cannot be redeemed. It is considered sold — period. Where real estate is concerned, the property may be redeemed within 180 days of the sale. The redemption price is the purchase price plus interest at the annual rate of 20 percent. See Code §6337(b). Payment must be made to the purchaser, and must be received by the purchaser within the 180-day grace period.

QUESTION 106
If I owe taxes, will I always have to deal with Automated Collection?

Automated Collection is a centralized collection office. They will send out the computerized notices, handle phone calls, and, in some cases, make collection calls. Most enforced collection action is taken by local revenue officers in the district where the citizen resides.

Once the case reaches a critical point — that is, where mere notices aren't generating any payment action — the case will usually be transferred to the district and revenue officers will be assigned to carry out collection.

If you are faced with a collection problem, rather than attempting to deal with Automated Collection which will do nothing but frustrate and enrage you, your time is better spent communicating with the local collection branch. At least this way, you'll be in touch with a person capable of making a decision on your case. With Automated Collection, all you'll get is a parrot reciting what the computer says you owe, and demanding immediate payment.

The local collection branch can be located by contacting the district director's office. Once you've gotten a phone number, any supervisor should be able to give you the name of the revenue officer who would be responsible to handle your case.

QUESTION 107
How should I pay taxes once Collection has the case?

Where it is possible, taxes should be paid in cash. Only a cash payment will put an immediate stop to all enforced collection action. Anything less than full payment will keep you under the thumb of the revenue officer on your case.

After payment is made, a receipt for the payment should be demanded. The receipt should show the amount paid, the date, the year in question and should bear the signature of the revenue officer taking the payment. This receipt may be needed later if you are ever questioned about making the payment.

QUESTION 108
After taxes are paid, will the liens be lifted?

IRS is supposed to file with the county registrar a Certificate of Release of Federal Tax lien when the taxes are paid. I have seen occasions, however, where these releases did not get filed. The best thing to do is demand the release at the time the tax is paid and hand carry it yourself to the registrar's office. This way, you can be sure the Certificate gets filed where it supposed to be filed. Only by filing the Certificate will the liens be released.

140 YOUR WORST FEARS

QUESTION 109
Can I enter into a payment agreement with the IRS?

The Collection Division has, by comparative standards, very few regulations which direct the actions of revenue officers. As a result, individual revenue officers have wide latitude and discretion in the collection function. They can accept or reject payment agreements on the basis of the facts of each case, or upon the "judgment" of the revenue officer involved.

After you have told the revenue officer that full payment of the tax cannot be made, and that you wish to make installment payments, you will be required to fill out a detailed financial statement disclosing all of your assets and liabilities. On the basis of the financial statement, the revenue officer will determine what the minimum installment is that you can afford and you will be expected to pay it. You may even be required to reduce other living expenses in order that more taxes can be paid. In one case, the IRS demanded that a couple take their three children out of private school in order that they then would be able to afford to pay more taxes.

You may also enter into a payroll deduction payment program, but in order to do this, your employer will have to be notified of the liability and participate in its collection. This may not have favorable ramifications.

Two other factors must be considered in deciding whether a payment agreement with the IRS is desirable. First, IRS charges interest at a floating rate, compounded daily. See Question 40. Because of this, a fixed rate, simple interest bank loan is likely to be substantially less expensive in the long run.

Secondly, the IRS has the power to terminate the payment agreement without notice to you if they determine that their revenue is in danger. Consequently, even though you have been making payments religiously, you may find yourself faced with a levy situation which appears "out of the blue."

This very thing occured in one case with which I am familiar. A tax of $17,000 was assessed against a person, and, in typical fashion, the IRS demanded full immediate payment. He went into the local collection office and explained that he had applied for a loan to pay the tax, but that it would take some time to get approved. In the meantime, he agreed to pay $1,000 per month until the loan went through, at which time the tax was to be paid in full. Before leaving the office, he made his first $1,000 installment.

Within 60 days, two more payments were made, but the loan still had not been approved. Then one day, without any notice whatsoever, and before the fourth payment was due to be made, the IRS levied his checking account, taking all of his money. At the time the levy was made, several checks were out but had not yet been presented to the bank for payment. By the time they were presented, there was no money in the account to cover them, and, of course, they all bounced.

This naturally upset the bank, whose initial reaction was that the person was writing bad checks all over town. It also happened to be the same bank to which he had applied for the loan. After seeing all of the bad checks and the IRS levy, they nearly refused to make the loan, claiming that their payments would be jeopardized by the IRS actions.

With this kind of behavior going on routinely, one wonders whether the IRS is in the business of collecting taxes, or financially destroying people. Had they left the man alone, he would have gotten the money from the bank much sooner then he finally did. Because of their "shotgun" approach to collection, more than one person has been financially ruined, preventing not only the collection of **all** taxes owed, but, in many cases, preventing collection of **any** taxes.

QUESTION 110
Can I negotiate the tax with Collection?

Code §7122 gives the IRS authority to "compromise" a tax. The term is not specifically defined in the Code or the regulations, but it is understood to mean that a lessor amount than has been assessed will be accepted as full payment. Two reasons are given as a basis to compromise a tax.[35]
The compromise can be based upon either a question of liability, or a question of collectability.

Where it can be shown that there is a doubt as to your actual liability for the amount assessed, a compromise can reduce the assessment to the amount you would legally owe. For example, suppose you received a notice of deficiency which disallowed all deductions for a particular year, and established a tax due based upon your gross income only. Naturally, without the benefit of any deductions to which you would be entitled, the deficiency would be greatly in excess of

---
[35] Rev. Reg. §301.7122-1(a).

what was shown on the return. Now, further suppose that for one reason or another, you didn't petition the Tax Court within the requisite 90-day grace period and the deficiency became an assessment.

Rather than paying the entire amount of the assessment, which is probably many times more than what you legally owe, you could make an offer to compromise the debt on the basis of your actual liability. You would then demonstrate to the revenue officer, on an Offer in Compromise Form (IRS Form 656) what your actual liability should be. Once this is done, the tax can be compromised to its proper level, eliminating the hardship of paying the excessive assessment.

The other reason to compromise is based upon your ability to pay the amount assessed. Where a tax has been assessed which is beyond your ability to pay, the IRS has the authority to reduce the tax to a manageable level. The ability to pay compromise is not based upon hardship or inconvenience, and therefore is not so readily accepted by the IRS. In order to effect a reduction of the liability for this reason, you must, at least on paper, be insolvent. When the IRS sees that the probability of collecting the full assessment is greatly reduced by virtue of a poor debt to equity ratio, they may well compromise the tax.

One beauty of an offer in compromise is that where a reasonable offer is made, and where the government's interests are not "jeopardized," collection action will frequently be stayed while the offer is being considered.[36] The stay is not automatic, but will be based upon the merits of the offer, and the good faith of the person making it. For this reason, the amount offered as the compromise should generally be paid when the offer is made.

The offer in compromise is a little known tax management tool which can greatly assist in bringing under control an out-of-control financial situtation. If you are faced with an excessive assessment, you'd do well to study the compromise statute and to make every effort to resolve your assessment through this process.

---

[36] Rev. Reg. §7122(d)(2).

QUESTION 111
How do I make an offer in compromise?

The offer itself is made on IRS Form 656. It must be accompanied with a financial statement (Form 433) and the amount which is offered as the compromise. In addition, where the compromise is based upon collectability, a collateral agreement is usually required. A collateral agreement (Form 2261) is executed by the debtor, who agrees to pay additional sums of money to the IRS out of future sources of income, or waives his right to any tax credits or refunds to which he may be entitled. The effect of the collateral agreement, then, is to increase the amount of money which the IRS will eventually get through its collection action.

Once the offer is accepted, the amount of tax liability is fixed and cannot be changed. The offer can be terminated, however, if payments under the offer are not made at the time or times required. And if the offer is rejected, you will be expected to pay the full amount of the assessment.

Chapter Four
UNDER THE GUN
Questions Relating to Criminal Investigation

Background to this Chapter —

The Criminal Investigation Division (CID) is the IRS police force. Special Agents, those who conduct the criminal investigation, are responsible to follow up allegations of criminal conduct on the part of citizens and businesses. Their primary job is to gather evidence and build the cases which are ultimately presented in court. CID will also gather evidence and build the case for the civil fraud penalty. See Question 39.

CID is the least desirable branch of the IRS family to become entangled with. When CID has jurisdiction of the case, it is because there has been an allegation somewhere by somebody that you have committed a criminal act in connection with your income tax responsibilities.

There is an important distinction between the kind of cases we have already discussed, and those handled by CID. Each of the cases we have discussed thus far in this work have been civil cases. CID involves itself only with criminal cases. The main difference between a civil and a criminal case is that in a criminal case the consequences of losing are that you could go to jail, as well as be fined.

Where civil cases are concerned, the consequences of failure are purely economic. That is, you can be forced to pay the back taxes, interest and some penalties based upon the amount of tax due. The prospect of jail never enteres into the picture in a civil case, but permeates the discussion of criminal cases.

The IRS — admittedly — is very selective as to who will be prosecuted for a tax offense. Relatively few criminal prosecutions are brought each year, but the conviction rate is high in those cases that are brought. Based upon these facts, we can safely conclude that the IRS will not bring a case unless they are certain it can be won. The reason is that IRS simply cannot afford to lose criminal cases. Whenever a criminal case is lost, the IRS is set back indeterminably in the establishment and maintenance of "presence." It cannot ever let the public believe that the IRS can be beaten in criminal tax cases. Once this notion gains any widespead acceptance, the lion loses its teeth.

I guess this is the reason special agents seem to be the most thorough of all IRS personnel. When involved in an investigation, special agents will leave no stone unturned. Literally, they will travel from one end of the United States to the other, if need be, to track down any leads they may have. By the time the case is ready for prosecution, they will have spoken to the citizen under investigation, his employer, those with whom he works, possibly his spouse and children, his friends and enemies, his banker and those with whom he does business.

When the case goes to trial, the IRS will know just about everything there is to know about the person "under the gun." They will know how much money he made for the years under investigation, how it was spent and where it was spent. They'll know whether he ran it through his bank account, took the money in cash, or sent it to a foreign bank outside the jurisdictional limits of the United States.

They will know whether he was boisterous about his actions, or was closed mouth about the going's on. They'll know whether and to what extent records were kept, and by whom, and to a large degree, whether or not they are accurate. In short, the criminal investigation spares no expenditure of time or money in the reconstruction of one's entire personal or business life **vis-a-vis** his income tax obligations.

It is true that the pinch of CID will be felt by fewer persons than will that of any other division we have discussed, but on the other side of the coin, the pinch of CID can be substantially more devastating and longlasting than that of the others. It is for that reason that we look deeply into CID at this time.

QUESTION 112
If I don't "evade" my taxes, why do I have to worry about a criminal prosecution?

The criminal prosecution is a very important weapon in the IRS' enforcement arsenal. Moreover, the prosecution plays a major role in the overall plan of establishing and maintaining "presence." Even before the Strategic Plan was issued, the IRS recognized that the successful prosecution of a person well known or respected in the community resulted in substantial "deterrent effect" in that district. For this reason, IRS has established as one of the selection criteria in criminal cases a consideration of the "impact and/or deterrent effect that a successful prosecution case will generate."[1]

You will also notice that many of the criminal tax prosecutions which take place in this country are brought in the spring of the year. Has it ever occurred to you that the reason criminal charges are made in March and early April of the year is that the individual return filing deadline is April 15th? With news of persons being charged with various tax crimes splattered across newspaper headlines, the IRS is likely to gain the mileage it desires, whether or not the accused citizen is ultimately convicted by a jury.

The mileage I speak of comes in the form of terrified citizens who are convinced that they had better knuckle under and do what the IRS says, **without complaint**, or they are likely to become next year's headlines. While it is true that this message is never communicated in plain English, it nevertheless is received loud and clear by the American public. If you don't believe it, just ask your neighbor what he thinks will happen if you don't pay your taxes. Without batting an eyelash he'll tell you: "Are you crazy!? You'll end up in jail."

The fact is very few cases of "tax fraud" are brought in a given year and not all those convicted "end up in jail." But you'd never know it by talking to the man-on-the-street. And just how do you think he came to that conclusion? He has drawn the conclusion because that is exactly what the IRS wants him to think, and that opinion is reinforced each and every year with the wide-spread publicity given those few who are unfortunate enough to find their names on a grand jury indictment.

In order to perpetuate this most effective advertising system, the IRS needs persons to prosecute. With the total elimination of any "tax fraud" publicity, the public awareness of the IRS' teeth will become greatly diminished and eventually, will disappear. The result will be more and more tax evasion or attempted tax evasion.

To combat this, the IRS conducts a very carefully orchestrated and subtly executed campaign of terror. They never refer to it in these terms, however. They refer to it as "encouraging and achieving the highest degree of voluntary

---

[1] See IR Manual Supplement 9G-93, January 10, 1979.

compliance with the tax laws by enforcing statutory sanctions."[2] Either way you say it, the procedure is the same — prosecute just enough citizens for tax crimes so that the resulting publicity terrorizes the general population into silently paying their taxes.

I will even go so far as to speculate that the IRS views a certain amount of tax cheating as "healthy" for the system. Before you irrevocably brand me a kook, let me explain. "Controlled cheating" does two things. First and most importantly, it provides the raw material for the publicity campaign which the IRS needs to establish and maintain "presence." Without cheating, there is nobody to prosecute, and with nobody to prosecute, there are no headlines. No headlines — no terror.

Secondly, most of those who cheat develop a guilty conscience as a result of doing so. A guilty conscience emasculates a person to the point where he will not speak out against the agency he believes to have cheated. The result is that even though most Americans believe that the IRS goes too far in the collection of taxes, they are incapable of doing anything about it, due in large part to the guilty conscience. Very simply, they are afraid to speak out for fear of the ramifications of being looked at too closely.

The product of these factors is that the IRS has nearly free rein to do what it wants to whomever it wants, with little or no fear of any worthwhile retaliation on the part of the citizens of the United States. The Plan inicates that this attitude will not only continue, but the IRS will step up its efforts to terrorize Americans by creating and maintaining "presence." The only possible way to do this is to increase audits, increase enforced collection practices, and yes, increase criminal prosecutions — not of "tax cheats" or the Big Three, since it is expected that these people will be prosecuted, but of the man on the street — you. Only by attacking the man-on-the-street will the remaining men on the street get the message that they had better toe the line without complaint.

QUESTION 113
What are the different types of tax offenses?
When we hear in the news of a person being charged or convicted of a tax offense, we always hear that he has been

---
[2] Ibid, 9G-93.

charged with "tax fraud" or "tax evasion." The truth is that "fraud" and "evasion" are only two in a series of offenses related to income taxes.

Some offenses are more serious than others in terms of their penalty, and some are more common than others in terms of their occurance. The following is a comprehensive discussion of the more common tax offenses, as well as the penalty for violation of the offense.

1. Attempted Evasion, §7201 — Under §7201, any person who willfully attempts "in any manner to evade or defeat any tax imposed by this title or the payment thereof, shall. . .be guilty of a felony." The penalty upon conviction can be up to 5 years in prison, together with a $100,000 fine ($500,000 for corporations) and the costs of prosecution.

To be convicted of the crime of "tax evasion," the government must prove that the defendant — the person charged with the crime — a) owed a tax to the government which was not paid, b) that he committed an affirmative act (as distinguished from an "act of omission"), to keep from paying the tax, and c) that he acted willfully.

2. Failure to File Return or Pay Tax, §7203 — §7203 provides that if any person required by the tax laws to pay any tax or to "make a return. . .keep any records, or supply any information, who willfully fails to pay such. . .tax, file such return, keep such records, or supply such information, at the time or times required by law, shall, in addition to other penalties provided by law, be guilty of a misdemeanor. . ."

The penalty for conviction of this misdemeanor offense is substantially less than that of the felony tax offenses. Conviction under §7203 will expose the defendant to one year in prison and a $25,000 fine ($100,000 for corporations), plus the costs of prosecution. But perhaps a more significant difference lies in the area of loss of civil liberties. A §7203 conviction will not result in loss of the right to vote, or to own firearms, etc., whereas a §7201, and other felony convictions does.

Although §7203 spells out four possible offenses, each one separate and distinct from the other, the most common cases involve failure to file returns and failure to pay taxes. For a failure to file prosecution to be successful, the government must show a) that a return was required to have been filed, b) that it was not filed at the time required, and c) that the failure to file was willful. A failure to pay conviction would require proof that a) a tax was due and owing, b) that it was not paid, and c) that the failure to pay was willful.

You'll notice that each of these offenses involves the failure to carry out an act which the law commands. This is referred to as an **act of omission**. What distinguishes the felony in §7201 from the misdemeanor in §7203 is this precise attribute. Under §7201, the government must prove that the defendant committed specific affirmative acts — **acts of commission** — in order to defeat the payment of the tax. Without such proof, any conviction would not be valid. Where the conduct involves merely failing to do an act the law requires, the less severe misdemeanor statute applies.[3]

3. Submission of False Withholding Statement, §7205 — This section relates to Forms W-4, Employee's Withholding Allowance Certificate, which is filed with an employer at the commencement of the term of employment.[4] Section 7205 holds that "Any individual required to supply information to his employer under section 3402 who willfully supplies false or fraudulent information, or who willfully fails to supply information thereunder which would require an increase in the tax to be withheld under section 3402, shall. . .be fined not more than $1,000, or imprisoned not more than 1 year, or both.''

Section 7205 is, like §7203, a misdemeanor offense. In order for a conviction under §7205 to be upheld, the government would have to prove a) that a false withholding certificate was filed by you with your employer, b) that you knew it was false when it was filed, and c) that you filed the form willfully, with the deliberate intent to mislead.

4. Submission of a False Document, §7206(1) — This statute is the perjury or false statement statute. It provides that any person who ''willfully makes and subscribes any return, statement or other document, which contains or is verified by a written declaration that it is made under the penalties of perjury, and which he does not believe to be true and correct as to every material matter. . .shall be guilty of a felony. . .'' The penalty for conviction of a perjury violation is three years in prison and a $100,000 fine ($500,000 for corporations), plus the costs of prosecution.

---

[3] **Spies v. United States**, 317 U.S. 492 (1942).
[4] See Code §§3401 and 3402.

A successful conviction under §7206(1) will require evidence of the following facts: a) that a return or statement was filed by you which contained the declaration that it was made under penalty of perjury, b) that the return or statement was false as to a matter which materially affected the information reported, c) that you knew it was false when you filed it, and d) that you filed the form willfully, with the deliberate intent to mislead. This statute is a felony, and if convicted of violating its provisions, you'll suffer the loss of civil rights incident to a felony conviction, as well as be subject to the penalty imposed by the statute.

5. Aiding and Abetting the Filing of a False Statement, §7206(2) — This statute is the tax preparer statute, and is designed to punish those responsible for preparing or assisting in the preparation of false returns, **whether or not** the person for whom the return was prepared actually knew it was false.

The law states that any person who "willfully aids or assists in, or procures, counsels, or advises the preparation or presentation under, or in connection with any matter arising under, the internal revenue laws, of a return, affidavit, claim, or other document, which is fraudulent or is false as to any material matter, whether or not such falsity or fraud is within the knowledge or consent of the person authorized or required to present such return, affidavit, claim or document. . ." is guilty of a felony and can be imprisoned up to three years and fined up to $100,000 ($500,000 for corporations), upon conviction.

A conviction under §7206(2) would require proof of the following facts: a) that you aided in or counselled in some way the preparation or presentation of a tax return, statement or claim which was false as to a material matter, b) that you knew it was false when it was submitted, and c) that your conduct was willful.

Each of the above statutes requires proof of certain facts before conviction of violating that statutue can be upheld. These separate facts are called elements. The government must prove each and every element of the offense charged "beyond a reasonable doubt" before the defendant can be convicted. If the government fails to prove just one element of the offense, then their entire case fails and the defendant would have to be found not guilty.

QUESTION 114
What does the term "willfullness" mean?

You no doubt have noticed that the one element which appears in each tax offense is the element of willfullness. Willfullness is a factual showing that must be made in each and every prosecution under the tax laws before a conviction can be obtained. We have already discussed the term in earlier topics[5] and the definition given the word in the criminal law is not substantially different from that already mentioned. In fact, the earlier definition we have discussed grows out of criminal cases.

To review, the term "willfullness," as it is used in the criminal tax laws, means a voluntary, intentional violation of known legal duty.[6] The requirement that wilfullness be proven is meant to prevent the conviction of a person who makes an honest mistake on his tax return, or due to negligence or some other non-criminal reason, does not do what the law requires. In order to be convicted of a tax offense, one must know what the law requires of him, and he must deliberately and intentionally set out to break the law.[7]

We have all heard the axiom which holds that ignorance of the law is no excuse. This saying applies **only** to offenses that are characterized to as **malum in se** in nature. **Malum in se** is a Latin phrase which means: "A wrong in itself; an act or case involving illegality from the very nature of the transaction, upon principles of natural, moral and public law.[8] Examples of such an offense would be theft, murder or rape.

Tax laws do not fall into this catagory. Rather, they are classified as offenses which are **malum prohibitum**. This Latin phrase means: "A wrong prohibited; a thing which is wrong **because** prohibited; an act which is not inherently immoral, but becomes so because its commission is expressly forbidden by positive law. . ."[9] This concept is the opposite of **malum in se**. Tax laws fall into the **malum prohibitum** category. That is to say, it is a crime not to pay taxes only because Congress has so declared it. It's not inherently immoral not to pay taxes, as it is to rob or murder somebody. Consequently, the government must prove a **specific intent** to

---
[5] See Questions 39 and 101.
[6] **United States v. Pomponio**, 429 U.S. 10 (1976).
[7] **United States v. Bishop**, 412 U.S. 346 (1973).
[8] Black's Law Dictionary, Fourth Edition.
[9] Ibid.

break a tax law. Such intent is a state of mind referred to as **mens rea**[10], which is defined as a guilty or wrongful purpose. Without proof of a guilty or wrongful purpose, a criminal tax conviction is improper.

One jurist put it this way: "Even a dog distinguishes between being stumbled over and being kicked."[11] As a consequence of these well-settled legal principles, no person should ever be convicted of violating the tax laws where his actions were merely negligent or grew out of a good faith misunderstanding of the requirements of the law. The criminal statutes apply only to the willfull or intentional violator, not the mistaken, mislead or negligent person.[12]

QUESTION 115
What is the difference between tax "evasion" and tax "avoidance"?

Much debate has focussed upon the nature and distinction between tax "evasion" and tax "avoidance." To put the terms in the their simplest context, it could be said that the **attempt**, whether or not successful, to reduce or eliminate one's taxes by means which are not legal, would constitute evasion. Avoidance, on the other hand, involves the structuring of one's financial affairs in such a fashion so as to pay as little tax as possible, so long as no violation of law occures in the process.

For decades the rich, through the use of astute tax counsel, have used trusts, corporations and other cleverly structured transactions to reduce or eliminate what they might have otherwise paid in taxes. So long as the transactions conform to the requirements of the law, there is no violation punishable under the criminal statutes. When one deliberately and willfully pays less tax then he knows is due, then fraud or evasion enters into the picture.

QUESTION 116
Is tax avoidance legal?

Perhaps the statement of Judge Learned Hand in **Helvaring v. Gregory**[13] best answers the question:

---

[10] Ibid.
[11] **Morissette v. United States,** 342 U.S. 246, at footnote 9 (1952).
[12] **United States v. Dahlstrom**, 713 F.2d 1423 (9th Cir. 1983).
[13] 69 F.2d 809, 810 (1932).

> "Anyone may so arrange his affairs that his taxes shall be as low as possible; he is not bound to choose that pattern which will best pay the Treasury; there is not even a patriotic duty to increase one's taxes."

In the same case on appeal to the Supreme Court[14], Justice George Sutherland declared:

> "The legal right of a taxpayer to decrease the amount of what otherwise would be his taxes, or altogether avoid them, by means which the law permits, cannot be doubted."

It is well settled that a person may, provided the means used are legal, avoid any part or all of his taxes. The trouble usually begins when the line is crossed into the grey area of transactions which are not clearly legal.

QUESTION 117
Is there a statute of limitations on tax offenses?

Code §6531 establishes a period of limitations after which no person can be "prosecuted, tried or punished for any of the various offenses arising under the internal revenue laws. . ." The general rule is that the period of limitations is three years, except in the case of eight exceptions to the rule. In those eight cases, the period of limitation is six years. Each of the criminal offenses we have discussed above falls into one of the eight exceptions to the three-year rule. Hence, the statute of limitations for prosecution of each offense we have discussed is six years.

QUESTION 118
What does the typical criminal investigation involve?

As we have said in the Background to this Chapter, once a criminal case comes to fruition, the IRS will have uncovered virtually every fact there is to know about the target of the investigation. This is because the typical investigation involves a look at nearly all aspects of the defendant's life.

The first thing the IRS will look at is all the financial data relative to the person under investigation. Past tax returns will be pulled and scrutinzed for further evidence of fraud, or

---

[14] **Gregory v. Helvering**, 293 U.S. 465 at page 469 (1934).

patterns in conduct. All bank records will be obtained through the process of the third party summons,[15] and where possible, the target himself will be questioned extensively, and his personal books and records will be looked at.

The books and records of any business in which the target was involved will be viewed, as well as all documents relative to the purchase and sale of real estate or other valuable property. The IRS will attempt to reconstruct each and every financial transaction to the fullest extent possible, in order to build an unassailable case.

In addition to the financial investigation, IRS will do an extensive investigation of your personal history. This will include a look at your eductional background and to a lesser extent, your physical condition. Your current physical condition may be a factor in determining whether you could withstand the "rigors of trial."

They will talk to your friends and enemies in an effort to reconstruct your business and personal dealings. Discussions with business associates and employees, and even family members will be conducted for the same purpose. It is not unusual for the IRS to mail what is called a canvass letter. This letter would be a form letter addressed to customers, employees or associates informing them that you are under investigation and encouraging them to contact the special agent to discuss their knowledge of your affairs. As you might imagine, such a letter has a devastating effect on one's business and personal life.

The unchecked power of CID to indiscriminately mail such letters has alone been responsible for destroying many businesses whose owners were never even charged with committing a criminal act. One case which comes to mind involves a man who sold small airplanes for a living. He conducted his affairs at a municipal airport in central Alabama.

After getting his bank records from a Montgomery bank, the special agent mailed canvass letters to all his customers, business associates and even suppliers.

Almost overnight, his business was ruined. After all, if given a choice, would you do business with a person you knew to be a target of an IRS criminal investigation? Nobody wants that kind of attention in their lives. Within a short

---

[15] See Questions 25 and 26.

period of time, the salesman was forced to dump his business to survive, though he was not charged with any crime. This tragedy is repeated regularly throughout the United States.

QUESTION 119
What in particular are Special Agents looking for?
Besides the obvious answer — unreported income — the IRS is looking for evidence of willfullness, or intent to break the law. Without it, they cannot convict the target of any wrongdoing. Generally speaking, banks and business records, and to a lesser extent, conversation with employees and associates, will be sufficient to prove the elements of the offense which relate to the transaction itself.

For example, in the case of failure to file a return, they will have bank or employment records to show how much income you received, and they have their own internal records to prove that no return was filed. These facts satisfy two of the three elements of the offense of failure to file.

What they lack is evidence of willfullness — specific intent to break the law. In an effort to find this kind of intangible evidence, they speak to as many people as possible and look at as many factors as possible, including personal history and business practices.

QUESTION 120
If I'm under criminal investigation, why can't I just pay the tax they think I owe?
Once the case is in the hands of a special agent, you cannot just "pay the tax" to end the criminal investigation. When a case is assigned to a special agent, the first thing he will do is to file a Form 4135, Criminal Control Notice. This form is sent to the Service Center serving the district in which the target resides. When the 4135 is received by the Service Center, they establish an "internal module freeze," referred to as a TC 914.

The module freeze is a freeze on the activities of the taxpayer's account with the IRS. This is internal in nature only, and you will not know it has happened. The effect of the module freeze is to vest total control of the case in the hands of the special agent. After the freeze is in place, no decisions are made on your case without his knowledge and imput. More importantly, no refunds are supposed to be made, and no tax payments are supposed to be credited to your account during the investigation.

If you went to the IRS — either the case agent or by letter to the Service Center — in an effort to pay a given amount of taxes during the criminal investigation, you will be told that your money cannot be posted to your account until the investigation has been completed and all criminal avenues have been pursued. Only then will you be allowed to pay any taxes.

As crazy as this sounds, it's the truth. In one case, the target of the investigation mailed a cashier's check in the amount of $10,000 to the IRS, with instructions that it be used to pay whatever they considered his tax liability for the years in question. They wrote back stating that since the investigation was pending, they could not credit the payment to his account. They gave him the option of either holding the money in a "suspense file" until the investigation was completed or returning it to him. He elected to have the money returned and they promptly did so.

Another consideration which comes into play here, and which warrants some discussion, is the "greed factor." In every criminal prosecution I've ever seen, the prosecutor will use as a key argument in his presentation to the jury the "greed factor." He will endeavor to paint the picture that the defendant is a greedy individual who "didn't want to pay his fair share of the income tax."

If the IRS were to allow criminal targets to pay taxes before the case went to trial, they would have effectively eliminated the "greed factor" as a principal means of securing convictions in criminal cases.

QUESTION 121
Which aspects of a tax case are decided first, the civil or criminal?

Almost without exception, the IRS will always pursue the criminal avenue in a case before they undertake civil collection. That is, where a case has possible criminal potential, they will conduct the kind of thorough investigation which we have already outlined to determine whether prosecution is warranted. Only after the prosecution has been abandoned, or has been successfully carried out, will civil collection come into play.

QUESTION 122
If I am prosecuted for a tax offense, am I still liable for civil penalties?

Once a criminal case has run its course, resulting in either a prosecution or, for some reason, no prosecution, the IRS will assert civil liabilities and penalties. This is done by mailing a notice of deficiency to you. At that point, you will bear the burden of proving that you don't owe what they say you owe.[16]

If you've been convicted of a particular crime, the civil fraud penalty[17] will be asserted and the Tax Court will consider the fact that you've already been convicted in the criminal trial as conclusive proof of fraud sufficient to sustain the penalty.

If you haven't been convicted, the IRS will bear the burden of proving with "clear and convincing evidence" that part or all of the underpayment was due to fraud.

QUESTION 123
What basis is used to determine who will be prosecuted?

You would be inclined to believe that all tax cheaters are prosecuted. This is not the case. IRS and Justice Department personnel have stated on more than one occasion in my presence that they cannot possibly prosecute all "tax cheaters" or "tax protesters." There are just too many. For this reason, the IRS must be selective in who is prosecuted.

The precise criteria for selecting those who will and will not be prosecuted are not fully known. We do know that the "probability of success" standard plays a very key role in making the decision. If the special agent is convinced that you are guilty of a given crime, but the evidence is not as abundant as prosecutorial standards call for, the chances are that you will not be prosecuted. Rather, the IRS will determine a deficiency and assert the civil fraud penalty. This alternative is elected because, in Tax Court, the standard of "clear and convincing evidence" is far less rigid and easier to meet than the "beyond a reasonable doubt" standard used in the criminal prosecution.

We also know that where the IRS perceives a person's actions as advocating violation of the tax laws for protest or other reasons, that person will be singled out for prosecution

---
[16] See Chapter Two.
[17] See Question 39.

more quickly than others in the district. Keep in mind that IRS has stated that the purpose of criminal prosecutions in large part is to deter others from disobeying the tax laws. In this context, those persons whose successful prosecution will have the greatest impact on "voluntary compliance" in the district are likely to be prosecuted first.

One further consideration which the IRS uses is the "dollars and cents" factor. How much tax has been "evaded" in terms of dollars and cents? The larger the figure of taxes evaded, the greater the likelihood of success in the prosecution. This is not to say, however, that only those with large tax bills are prosecuted. In some cases, where the conviction will have a large impact on voluntary compliance, the IRS may prosecute where there are relatively few tax dollars involved.

QUESTION 124
How is the typical criminal investigation begun?

There are two ways in which a criminal investigation can come into being. The first and probably most common way grows out of a routine audit.

During the course of such an audit, the revenue agent will come across something in the return which he believes to be indicative of fraud. Not that the revenue agent makes a determination that the law has in fact been violated, but he sees something that just doesn't look right. This may take the form of the existence of unreported income, or excessive deductions which cannot be proven. Any number of indicators may trigger in his mind the possibility of fraud.

Having raised such a flag, the revenue agent will refer the case to the Criminal Investigation Division. After initial analysis by CID of the evidence already in the hands of the IRS, the decision to run a full-scale investigation is made. Assuming the decision is to go ahead with the investigation, a special agent will be assigned to the case and from that point forward he will have total control of the direction the case is to take. The revenue agent will remain on the case and assist the special agent in what they term a "joint investigation."

The "joint investigation" is a bifurcated investigation which looks coterminously at the civil and criminal aspects of the case, with the criminal aspects taking precedent over the civil.

After the special agent has been assigned, he will file the Form 4135, Criminal Control Notice. The 4135 establishes the

TC 914 module freeze at the Service Center. Although the target of the investigation does not yet know it, he is the subject of a full-scale criminal investigation which will not be abandoned unless and until the special agent is convinced that sufficient evidence to convict the target cannot be found.

The second way a criminal investigation is begun grows out of the Service Center. Teams of trained personnel located at the Service Center review all incoming tax returns and documents to be sure that, at least superficially, they meet all the requirements of a "proper" tax form.

1040's must be signed, they must have W-2's attached, and, where necessary, they must have checks for taxes included. The teams review the forms to make sure all of these items, including the necessary schedules, are made a part of the return. What they are especially watchful for is what the IRS refers to as "non-processable documents." These "documents" generally take the form of some type of "protest" tax return.

A protest tax return is any return which IRS believes is filed as a means of protesting the income tax laws of the United States. Over the years, the number of protest returns received at the various Service Centers throughout the United States has greatly increased.[18] Any return which does not comport in all respects to a normal, conventional return, is treated as a "non-processable document," and labeled a protest return.

Such a return is routed away from the typical processing procedures, which include the imputation of the data on the return into the central computer. Instead, the "document" is sent to the Compliance Division of the Service Center, and under the direction of the Chief, Criminal Investigation Branch, correspondence with the "protestor" will be commenced.

Initial correspondence consists of a letter warning the citizen that the return which he has filed is not a proper tax return, and that a correct document should be filed at once. After 30 days have expired, if no answer or some form of unsatisfactory answer is received, the Chief, CIB will prepare a Form 3949, Intelligence Information Item. It is on this form that the initial determination is made whether additional investigatory research will be done, or whether the case will be routed to either Examination or Collection for civil collection action.

---

[18] Report by the Comptroller General of the United States, **Illegal Tax Protestors Threaten Tax System**, July 8, 1981.

Assuming the former course is elected, your case is sent to the Chief of the Criminal Investigation Division in the district where the citizen resides, and a second review of the file is made. The Chief, CID, makes a determination on the "impact and/or deterrent effect" that a successful prosecution case will have on voluntary compliance in the district. The next step, then, would be to assign a special agent for full scale investigation.

Where no tax return has been filed, Service Center computers, programmed to compare information returns, such as W-2's and 1099's, with 1040 Forms, search the files to discover whether tax returns have been filed by those apparently required to do so.

Where it is discovered that W-2's have been filed indicating the receipt of what the IRS would call income, but no 1040 has been filed, correspondence of the nature we have just discussed is sent to the citizen, and follow up is done in the fashion we have just outlined.

QUESTION 125
When will I learn that I'm under criminal investigation?

The first step the special agent will take in terms of actually accumulating evidence will be to contact the target and attempt to talk to him. This contact is always unannounced, and is done at most inopportune times and places. For example, it would not be unusual for two special agents (there will always be two special agents when contact with the target or other witnesses is made) to arrive at your home some morning at 7:30, just as you've gotten out of the shower. Or, they may show up at your place of employment, and, after they've announced to everybody in the office that they are special agents with Internal Revenue Service, demand to talk with you.

Once face-to-face with the target, they will read your rights to you. It sounds something like this:

> Mr. Yukvitz, my name is Larry Schmultz and I am a special agent with the Criminal Investigation Division of the Internal Revenue Service. As a special agent, one of my functions is to investigate possible violations of the tax and other criminal statutes. In connection with my investigation, I would like to ask you some questions, but before I do so, I must advise you that anything you say

to me can and will be used against you in any subsequent civil or criminal litigation. You have the right to remain silent, and you have the right to have an attorney present with you during questioning. Do you understand these rights? Now Mr. Yukvitz, (showing you a document) is that your signature on the bottom of that tax return?

Having been contacted by a special agent, and having been read your rights in the fashion I have just shown, it wouldn't take too much thought to come to the conclusion that you are under criminal investigation. In every criminal investigation that I have any familiarity with, the initial contact by the special agent with the target has occurred in this fashion.

QUESTION 126
Should I answer any questions asked by the special agent?

You judge for yourself after considering these ideas: The initial contact is a carefully planned and executed experience designed to catch you off-guard, and, hence, to elicit as much information from you as possible. Consider these various aspects of the contact:

First, you are not under arrest when the contact is made. Consequently, the Miranda-type warning you've been given is not required by law. This warning is required only when you are in custody. Why then is the warning given? I don't think it's to do you any favors. I believe they give the warning because hearing it scares the heck out of the listener. The mind races with confusion and immediately jumps to the worst possible conclusions — "I'm going to jail!" You are thus unable to think clearly during the course of the interview, if you consent to it.

Secondly, they arrive at your home or office completely unannounced, with no prior warning whatsoever. One minute you're addressing the problems of the moment, and the next, you're confronted with your tax return of probably two or more years previous, and are being questioned about it by federal agents. I once asked a special agent why they never set an appointment with the citizen before cornering him for questioning. His response was that "surprise encourages spontaneity on the part of the taxpayer." Of course it does, but the problem, especially for the "taxpayer," is that a spontaneous response is not always a correct response. This is particularly true when taken by complete surprise by law enforcement agents, and where you are questioned about matters which took place several years previous.

Remember, you will be questioned about events which took place in your life years before this interview. You have no records in front of you from which to refresh your memory, and you aren't given an opportunity to go back through your books to review just what you did why you did it. Questions are nevertheless rattled off one after the other. Couple this with the fear and confusion that has set in — if you're human — and the result is that it is nearly impossible to make completely accurate statements about your actions and state of mind.

In the meantime, the second agent is writing notes about everything that you say. Those notes will later be transcribed and put in the form a "Memorandum of Interview," which the agents will use as part of the evidence in your case. Later on, during the trial of your case (if it goes that far) you may wish to take the witness stand to testify in your own behalf.[19] You would testify to a series of events which you now recall quite well because you've had a chance, with a clear head, to review all the facts. Your account of the events as given from the witness stand very well could differ, either slightly or substantially, from that reported to the special agents. In fact, the government prosecutor is relying on it.

When this does happen, the prosecutor, on cross-examination, confronts you with those earlier statements which are now inconsistent with your present testimony. He jumps on you, making your every word appear as a lesson in fictional writing. The more you attempt to explain the inconsistencies, the worse you look to the jury. The result? Even though you've been completely truthful and honest in both situations — the only difference being your ability to accurately recall the facts — you've been shown to be a liar.

Many have made the mistake of believing that special agents will be understanding of the problem and that all one need do is to tell the truth and everything will be all right; that will be the end of it. It's just not that simple. Special agents are professional, highly trained criminal investigators who know exactly what evidence they need and exactly how to get it. In most every criminal prosecution I have seen, the most damning

---

[19] A defendant in a criminal case is not required to testify in his own trial. The decision to testify must be made at the time of being confronted with the question.

evidence against the defendant has been that which the defendant himself has given to the IRS out of his own mouth. Statements which you believe to be perfectly harmless and completely truthful, usually somehow come back to haunt you.

QUESTION 127
If I choose not to answer any of his questions, what should I tell him?

Experience has shown that the best way to deal with the unannounced special agent is to politely explain that under the circumstances you'd best not make any statement at this time. Suggest that if he put his questions in writing and send them to you, you'd consult counsel and provide a prompt written response to each question.

By doing this, you will have escaped the possible entrapment of "spontaneous" reponses without being rude or evasive. At the same time, if the agent cares to follow up in writing, you're assured of the opportunity to prevent any confusion or miscommunication by putting your answers in writing after discussing the matter with experienced counsel.

QUESTION 128
When can I have my counsel present with me?

At any time during the investigation, if you are being questioned by a criminal investigator or other IRS personnel in connection with the investigation, you have the right to counsel present with you. You can never be forced to make any statements either with or without counsel present.

QUESTION 129
How long does a criminal investigation take?

This is like asking how much it costs to buy a car. The answer depends on various factors. I've seen investigations take as long as four years, and as short as a few months. The longest investigation I've seen involved several individuals who were eventually charged with filing false income tax returns and conspiracy to defraud the government. There were 13 persons targeted and several special agents running the investigation. The investigation traced hundreds of transactions of every description which took place in various locations throughout the United States. The subsequent trial turned out to be, to my knowledge, the longest tax trial in the history of the United States. It lasted over 19 weeks and involved — at one time or another — a dozen defense lawyers, a half dozen prosecutors, hundreds of witnesses and many thousands of pages of documentary evidence.

The shortest investigation involved a Michigan man who was the self-styled leader of the local tax protest movement. The investigation began and ended in the spring of the year in the early 1980's. This was during the period when Detroit area automakers were flooded with workers exempting themselves from withholding by filing "exempt" Forms W-4. Obviously, the purpose of the prosecution was to discourage those participating in the tax movement by convicting their leader, which is exactly what happened.

QUESTION 130
What will happen when the special agent has completed his investigation?

Once all evidentiary leads have been ran-down, the special agent will write a report and make a recommendation. The recommendation is either 1) the criminal case should be dropped and the matter be referred to civil channels for tax collection, or 2) the target should be prosecuted for whatever violations the agent feels the evidence supports.

When prosecution is recommended, the agent will provide detailed findings with his recommedation. These findings summarize all of the evidence he has found during the course of the investigation, and how this evidence proves which laws he believes have been violated. He will identify all of the witnesses he has talked to, and, if he has talked to the target, he will set forth the details of all conversations. The report is a kind of blueprint for the prosecution of the case. All evidence, both pro and con, is considered in the special agent's analysis of the case.

The recommendation for prosecution, along with the detailed report, goes to the Office of District Counsel. You will recall from the last Chapter that District Counsel is the staff of attorneys who work solely for the IRS.

QUESTION 131
What role does District Counsel play?

In the context of a recommendation for prosecution, District Counsel will carefully review the special agent's report and recommendation. Being lawyers, they will look at the report and the evidence it summarizes from a legal standpoint. The question they ask themselves is whether the evidence which the agent has gathered is sufficient to convict the defendant of the crime he is believed to have committed. They will then ask themselves whether, after conviction, a court of appeals will agree that the evidence was sufficient.

In this way, District Counsel will play the role of defense counsel. They will anticipate defenses to the charges and consider whether the evidence is enough to overcome those defenses. In some cases, District Counsel will send a letter to the target inviting him to appear at a conference to discuss the case.

QUESTION 132
Will I be notified if the Special Agent has referred my case to District Counsel?

Generally, a letter is sent to the target when a case is referred to District Counsel. While not overly informative, it will tell you that the case has been forwarded to them for their consideration. The letter may or may not stipulate that you have been recommended for prosecution. Whether or not it does is irrelevant. The reality is that during a criminal investigation, District Counsel comes into the picture only if prosecution has been recommended.

QUESTION 133
Should I meet with District Counsel if I am invited to confer with them?

There are several considerations to keep in mind in deciding whether to meet with District Counsel if invited.

The first thing to realize is that District Counsel will have the special agent's complete report in their hands and will have copiously reviewed it prior to the conference. During the session, they will have the opportunity to ask you any and all questions which come to mind concerning the evidence they have before them. Secondly, to the extent that they have no evidence on a particular subject — the element of willfullness for example — their questions to you may very well be calculated to elicit such evidence.

The next thing to realize is that District Counsel will not entertain plea bargains at this point; nor will they consider pre-indictment settlement in any context. Therefore, it will do you no good to present yourself at the meeting looking for mercy or forgiveness in exchange for paying the tax they say you owe. What they are after more than anything else is to pick your brain to learn the nature of your defense.

The fourth and probably most important consideration to be cognizant of is that any statements made by you at the conference, like those made to the special agent, can and will be used against you by the IRS. Even those statements made by your counsel will be attributed to you in all respects. Therefore, if you do decide to appear at the conference with counsel, you will do well to have an understanding before hand as to what your counsel can and cannot say to the IRS lawyers. Anything he does say will stick to you like glue. See Question 41.

QUESTION 134
What will District Counsel do with the case after they've evaluated it?

After the case has been evaluated completely, including consideration of what they have gleaned at their conference with the target if one was held, they will decided whether to approve or reject the agent's recommendation for prosecution.

If they have rejected the recommendation on the basis of lack of evidence, the special agent may investigate further in an effort to fill the void uncovered by the lawyers. If the rejection is because they simply do not agree that the case can or should be carried forward, the matter will be dropped and the case will undertake a civil character.

If they approve the agent's recommendation, District Counsel will make a report and recommendation of their own. Their report goes to the United States Department of Justice, Criminal Tax Division in Washington, D.C. There, Justice Department tax attorney's review the entire file. The transmittal of the report from District Counsel to the Justice Department is referred to as a "formal recommendation for prosecution."

"Justice" has the final word on whether and to what extent a person will be prosecuted for tax violations. In reviewing the case, they will look for the same things District Counsel was interested in. The main difference is that Justice Department lawyers, unlike District Counsel lawyers, are seasoned prosecutors who have countless hours of courtroom experience. Since District Counsel attorneys practice mainly in Tax Court, they do not have the kind of field experience that the Washington prosecutors have. As a result, Justice is able to look at the case somewhat more objectively than is District Counsel, and they are better able to anticipate defenses to and problems with their case.

QUESTION 135
Will I be notified if District Counsel makes a formal recommendation for prosecution in my case?

If the case is referred to Washington, you will receive a letter from District Counsel, but it will not necessarily tell you that you have been "formally recommended for criminal prosecution." I have seen many letters to targets which simply say that "your case has been referred to the Justice Department for its consideration on this date." Without any background on what this means, the individual has no idea that he has been formally recommended for criminal prosecution.

Other such letters may specify exactly what it means to have one's case "referred to the Justice Department," and may even include a brief explanation of the precise laws which you are alleged to have violated.

Whether or not you are told by District Counsel why your case is headed to the Justice Department, you can be assured that there is only one reason such a referral ever takes place. That is to secure permission to go ahead with a prosecution for violation of one or more criminal tax statutes for one or more tax years.

QUESTION 136
Can the Justice Department reject the recommendation for prosecution?

As has been said, the Justice Department has the final word on whether and to what extent a person will be prosecuted for tax offenses. Consequently, they have the power to reject any recommendation for prosecution. Although I have no statistics on the number of cases that are approved versus those which are rejected, I will venture a guess that they reject the recommendation in very few cases. In my experience, though, I have seen it happen more than once.

QUESTION 137
Will I be notified if Justice approves the recommendation?

In time, you will be notified that Justice has approved the recommendation. The notice will come in any one of several forms. First, you may be invited to testify before a grand jury empanelled to consider whether you should be indicted for violation of one or more tax offenses. If you receive such a notice, the Justice Department has indeed approved the recommendation and the matter has gone to the next step.

Other notices may take the form of a summons to appear before a United States Magistrate for a bond hearing. In such a case, you have been charged with a federal crime and are now being brought before the courts to answer for it.

Still another notice may come in the form of an arrest. Special agents, probably the same ones who investigated you, may appear at your home or more likely, your place of employment, to arrest you for violation of one or more federal tax laws. In this situation, you'll be taken to the local jail and held there until you can appear before a Magistrate to set bond.

QUESTION 138
What is a grand jury?

A grand jury is a body of citizens empanelled to consider whether a person should be formally charged with and held to answer for violation of federal laws. There are two methods of charging a person with a crime in the United States.

The first is to charge by way of "information." An information is a document signed by the United States Attorney which alleges that a crime has been committed. It is supposed to be based upon an affidavit in the possession of the U.S. Attorney. The affidavit would state that the special agent has conducted an investigation and has found evidence to support the belief that you are guilty of violating one or more of the tax laws.

A criminal case can be commenced by way of information only where the crime charged is a misdemeanor, such as failure to file a tax return. See Question 113.

The next method of commencing a criminal prosecution is to charge by way of "indictment." An indictment is a finding by the grand jury that there is "probable cause" to believe that a crime has been committed and that you committed it. Probable cause is defined as evidence sufficent to "arouse suspicion" in a reasonable person that a crime was committed and that you committed it. Note that the finding of probable cause is not a finding of guilt. It merely means that suspicion has been raised to such a level that you must be held to answer for the charge.

All felony offenses must be charged by indictment. They cannot be brought by information. However, misdemeanor charges can be brought either by indictment or information.

QUESTION 139
Do I have the right to appear before the grand jury?

The grand jury is supposed to function as a completely independent body, apart from the Courts and the United States Attorney's Office. They have the power to investigate any allegation of wrongdoing on the part of any person or organization, and the power to command the appearance of any person to give testimony to assist them in their investigation.

The reality is that the grand jury is almost totally under the thumb of the prosecution's office. This is so because the only attorney who will be present during the grand jury's "secret" hearings is the United States Attorney assigned to the case. Even when a witness, such as the person under investigation, has been summoned to appear before the grand jury, his attorney cannot be present with him in the hearing room to give advice and counsel on the matters inquired into.

As a result of this control exerted by the prosecutor's office over the grand jury, it is safe to say that you will not be given an opportunity to testify before the grand jury unless the prosecutor wishes that you testify before the grand jury. If he has no desire that you do so, you will neither be directly informed that the investigation is pending, nor will you be invited or summoned to appear before them.

On the other hand, if it is determined that it is desirable to have you testify, you will either receive a letter "inviting" you to appear before them at a given time and date, or you will be subpoenaed to appear before them.

In either event, you will not be afforded an opportunity to have your own counsel with you in the hearing room. If you bring counsel, he will be forced to wait in the hall until the hearing is finished. If you have questions of him, you may leave the grand jury room, go into the hall and ask your counsel for advice, and return to the grand jury room to continue with your testimony. Moreover, the format of the grand jury hearing is such that you will simply answer the questions which have been put to you the by United States Attorney. There is the possibility that you may be given the privilege of making a brief statement before you leave, but the majority of your testimony will consist only of answering the prosecutor's questions posed in the context of a cross-examination. You are also subject to questioning by any or all of the grand jury members.

QUESTION 140
Can my grand jury testimony be used against me in my trial?

Absolutely. In fact, one major source of statements used as evidence against a defendant is his grand jury testimony. In tax cases, it is rare that any substantial extrinsic evidence of criminal intent, or willfullness, on the part of the accused exists. More times than not, the majority of evidence of criminal intent on the part of the defendant comes out of his own mouth.

This is why special agents will always attempt to talk with the target of an investigation, and why in tax cases it is not unusual for the target to be "invited" to testify before the grand jury. The result is pages and pages of statements which can be used against the defendant in his subsequent trial.

You may say, "Well, if I didn't do anything wrong, why do I have to worry about my statements being used against me?" Where grand juries are concerned, it's not that simple. The reason is that all questions are asked in the context of a cross-examination, mostly by the government attorney who will prosecute the case, and to a lesser extent, by the grand jurors themselves. Secondly, you do not have counsel with you upon whom you can rely for advice during the proceeding. If you waive your 5th Amendment rights, you can be forced to answer any question, whether or not that question would be allowed during the trial of your case, simply because you don't have counsel there to object to the question.

And lastly, and probably most significantly, since the grand jury is not an "adversarial proceeding[20] like a trial is, all of

---

[20] An adversarial proceeding is one where two opposing sides of a controversy are represented and have a chance to present their respective views before a decision is rendered.

your statements will be cast by the government attorney in a light most favorable to the government. Said another way, the grand jury will hear only the government's side of the story. While they will have your statements before them, the prosecutor will draw only those inferences from those statements which go to support the government's view of the facts. Your side of the case will never get presented to the grand jury.

QUESTION 141
What will happen if the grand jury decides to indict me?

If the grand jury agrees that there is probable cause to believe that a crime has been committed and that you committed it, they will formally charge you with that crime. The grand jury's act of charging a crime is called an indictment. If you are indicted, the case will be lodged with the local clerk of the United States District Court, and a file will be opened.

After that happens, notice that you've been indicted will come to you in one of two ways. You will either be arrested and brought to the federal courthouse to make bond, or you will receive a summons in the mail commanding that you present yourself at the federal courthouse to make bond. In either case, you will receive a copy of the indictment which will set out in detail the specific crimes that your are accused of committing.

QUESTION 142
How long before I am brought to trial?

In a criminal case, you can expect to be brought to trial within 70 days of the date of your first appearance at the courthouse. Section 3161 of the U.S. Criminal Code[21] is referred to as the Speedy Trial Act. It requires the trial of any criminal case to take place within that time period. The Speedy Trial Act was passed by Congress in the late 1970's in order that criminal defendants would be assured of their right to a speedy trial as set out in the 6th Amendment to the United States Constitution.

On its face, this may seem like a noble move on the part of Congress, but not so in application. For example, it is not

---
[21] See 18 USC §3161.

uncommon that trials in criminal cases take place anywhere from 40 to 50 days after the first appearance. Now, before you say "so what?" let's put this into perspective.

The IRS and the prosecutor's office have had anywhere from 6 months to 2 years — sometimes more — to prepare their case for prosecution. Now the defendant has only — at best — 70 days to prepare his case for the defense. Needless to say, this imbalance is grossly inequitable, weighing heavily in favor of the prosecution.

What is particularly interesting about the Speedy Trial Act is that it appears to be the only Constitutional right which you cannot waive. Any other constitutional right available to a criminal defendant can be waived. For example, you can waive your right to counsel, your right to confront the witnesses against you, your right to make a defense to the charges, or your right to an appeal. You can even waive your right to any trial at all, but you cannot waive you right to a "speedy" trial, even if you need more time to adequately prepare your defense. You are entitled to to a speedy trial and, by God, that's exactly what you're going to get!

QUESTION 143
What should I do if I am charged with a crime?

The charge of violating federal criminal tax laws is not an event which should be taken lightly. It is very serious and must be confronted that way. Decisions regarding your course of action in regard to a tax crime should not be made alone. Experience has shown that once a person has been charged with a crime, his internal "computer" jams. He is no longer able to make objective decisions about his case. He must have assistance.

It is quite possible, and I have seen it done, where persons have represented themselves in criminal cases and have done as good a job, if not better, than most attorneys could do. However, one is only able to do so as a result of months of preparation in **anticipation** of the charge.

If you are not prepared to represent yourself **before** being charged with a tax offense, it is impossible to get ready to do so **after** you've been charged. This is so for two reasons. The first is the time factor. Seventy days just doesn't give you enough time to prepare all that must be prepared to present an effective defense.

Secondly, because of the fact that your name is the one on the indictment, human nature is such that you become preoccupied with your exposure to fine and imprisonment if convicted. Rather than concentrating on trial preparation, you're concerned only with how much time you'll have to spend in prison if you lose. As a result, no expressive preparation is accomplished. Your only recourse under these circumstances is to hire competent, experienced counsel to assist in your defense.

QUESTION 144
If you were to diagram the criminal investigatory process, what would it look like?

A diagram of the process of a criminal investigation is shown in Figure 3.

Figure Three
Progression of Criminal Investigation

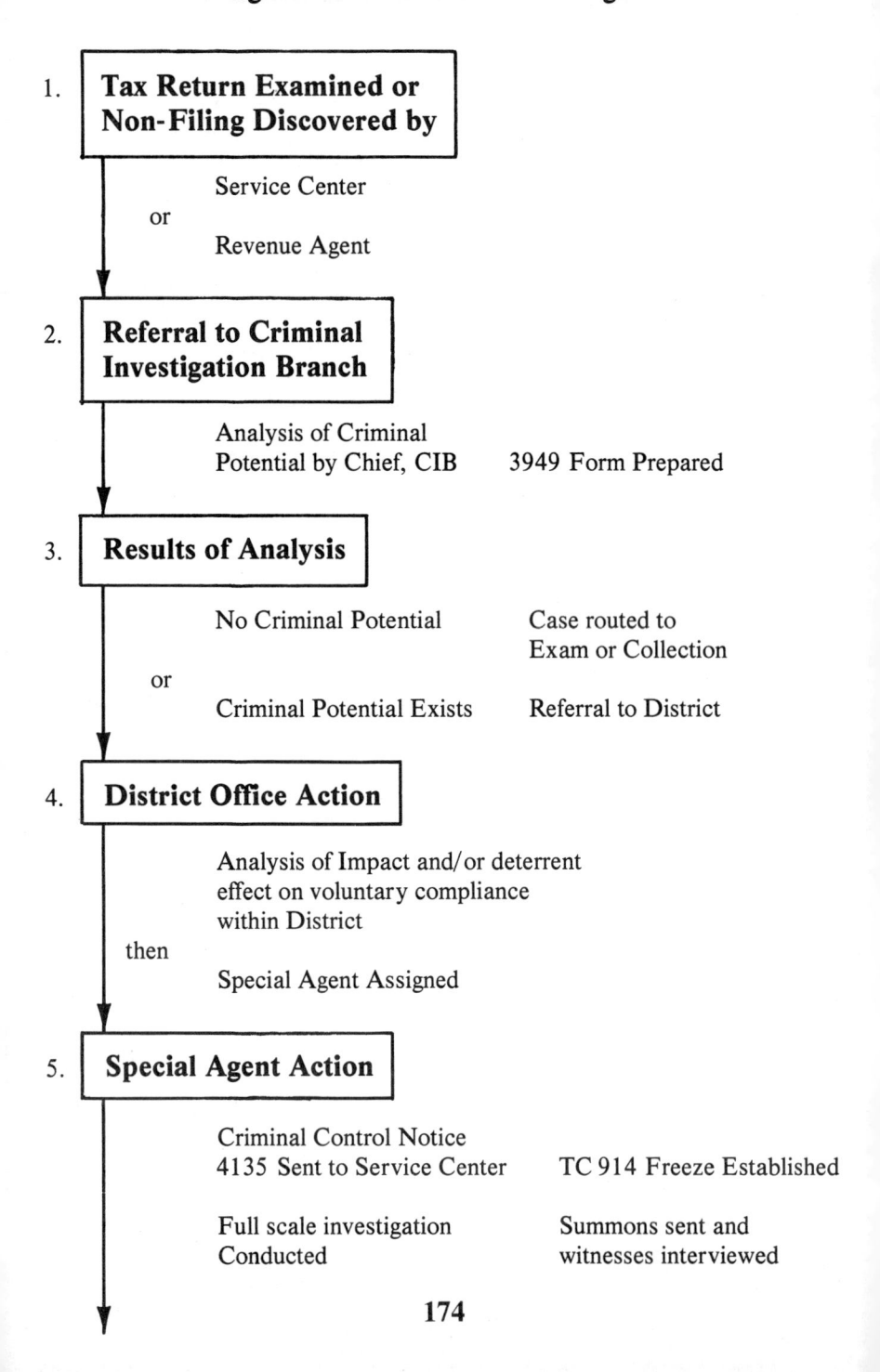

1. **Tax Return Examined or Non-Filing Discovered by**

   or   Service Center

   Revenue Agent

2. **Referral to Criminal Investigation Branch**

   Analysis of Criminal Potential by Chief, CIB   3949 Form Prepared

3. **Results of Analysis**

   No Criminal Potential   Case routed to Exam or Collection

   or

   Criminal Potential Exists   Referral to District

4. **District Office Action**

   Analysis of Impact and/or deterrent effect on voluntary compliance within District

   then

   Special Agent Assigned

5. **Special Agent Action**

   Criminal Control Notice
   4135 Sent to Service Center   TC 914 Freeze Established

   Full scale investigation   Summons sent and
   Conducted   witnesses interviewed

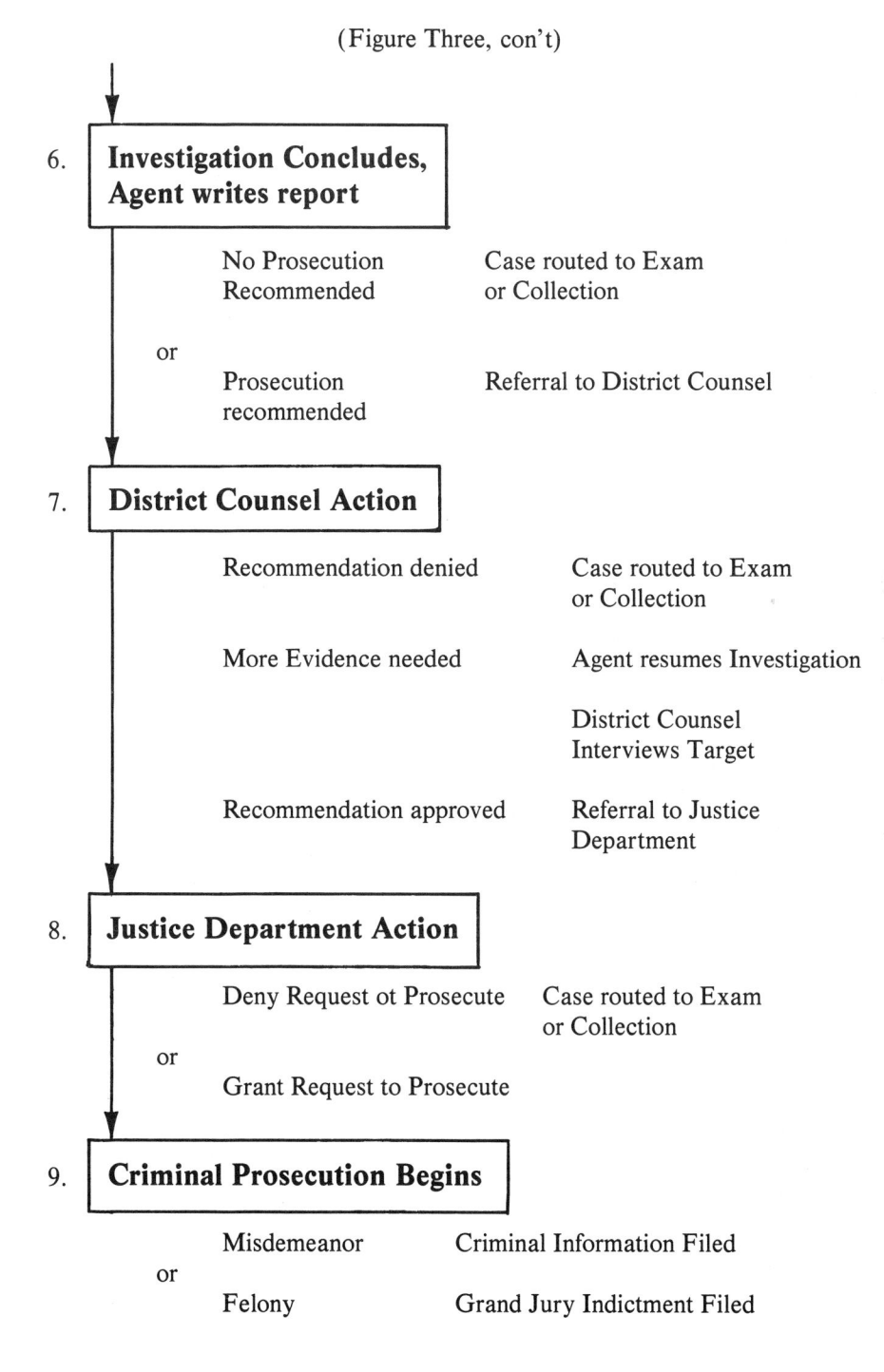

(Figure Three, con't)

6. **Investigation Concludes, Agent writes report**

    No Prosecution Recommended   Case routed to Exam or Collection

  or

    Prosecution recommended   Referral to District Counsel

7. **District Counsel Action**

    Recommendation denied   Case routed to Exam or Collection

    More Evidence needed   Agent resumes Investigation

                                   District Counsel Interviews Target

    Recommendation approved   Referral to Justice Department

8. **Justice Department Action**

    Deny Request ot Prosecute   Case routed to Exam or Collection

  or

    Grant Request to Prosecute

9. **Criminal Prosecution Begins**

    Misdemeanor   Criminal Information Filed

  or

    Felony   Grand Jury Indictment Filed

Chapter Five
UNTANGLING THE IRS
Miscellaneous Questions and Answers

Background to this Chapter —
To this point in our dissection of the IRS, we have dealt with very specific problems of what we might call an internal character. That is to say, those problems which arise when dealing directly with the IRS. There is an entirely different class of situations which we have not yet discussed, and which we could call problems of an external character.

These problems arise when dealing with others, and in which the affairs directly or indirectly involve the IRS. One obvious example is the relationship between you and your employer. I would be remiss if we didn't discuss the factors involving the interplay between you and your employer **vis-a-vis** the IRS.

The second general area with which we will be concerned is the organizational structure of the IRS. The structure of the IRS will be looked at in more of an informational then a strategical context. That is to say, I don't think any stunning upper hand is to be gained by knowing the fashion in which the IRS is organized, but, on the other hand, knowledge is power. To this end, I feel it apropos to look behind every drapery hung in the IRS mansion.

QUESTION 145
The IRS has never before posed any problem in my dealings with third parties. Why should I be concerned all of a sudden?

The one area of the Plan which is to me the most intriguing is that portion which calls for the "paperless tax return" within five to 10 years. In order that we have a "workable" system of electronic reporting and computation of tax liability without the need to mail a detailed report to the IRS, they must have already obtained the information from third party sources. It is in the achievement of this goal that we will find the IRS interfering with our third-party relationships on a rapidly increasing basis.

The concept of a "paperless tax return," or, more accurately, the idea that each person in our society will be reporting the transactions of those with whom he does business, is not so far-fetched. For example, the IRS has for some time required every person to report payments in excess of $600 made to any other person in the course of day-to-day business. Also, the Currency and Foreign Transactions Reporting Act[1] has, since 1973, required domestic banks and other financial institutions to report to the IRS any cash transaction involving currency of $10,000 or more in a single transaction. The IRS now wants this amount reduced to $3,000. Transfers of cash to foreign countries in excess of $5,000 are also required to be reported.

With each passing year, the transaction reporting requirements get more and more exotic and inclusive. The Tax Equity and Fiscal Responsibility Act of 1982 saw the addition of reporting requirements for persons involved in direct, multi-level sales, such as Amway or Shaklee. Under this new statute[2], any person involved in direct sales who has sales in excess of $5,000 for any one year must report the names, etc., of persons who purchased products wholesale, and to whom commissions were paid. And recently, we have seen the establishment of the requirement that **any person** must report to the IRS when paid cash in the amount of $10,000 in any one transaction. This requirement applies whether or not the $10,000 was paid in a single lump sum, or was paid in installments. If the aggregate equals or exceeds $10,000 and was paid in currency in any one taxable year, then the requirement to report the payment arises.[3]

As the machinery is set in place to require reporting of every transaction by every person, the IRS will have available the means of preparing a "paperless tax return" on your behalf. With each passing year, the financial dragnet gets broader and broader, and more and more persons and institutions are caught in its web. The result is that your affairs with others will have undertones directly related to the IRS. Not only will IRS have succeeded in making the "paperless tax return" possible, but will have established the ubiquitous "presence" called for in the Plan.

---

[1] See 31 USC §§1051-1122, and IRS Form 4789, Currency Transaction Report.
[2] See 26 USC §6041A.
[3] See 26 USC §6050I(a).

QUESTION 146
What do I report to my Employer on Form W-4?

The involvement of the IRS in third party affairs is no more prevalent than in the employer-employee relationship. The concept of wage withholding, or as the IRS refers to it, the "collection of income taxes at the source," came into existence in 1943, when the Victory Tax Act was passed into law. During America's involvement in the Second World War, Congress sold to the public the idea of regular wage withholding measures as a vehicle to more quickly collect revenues to prosecute the war. The idea was accepted because Congress and the President assured the public that the withholding measures were purely temporary and would be terminated after the war had ended. They of course were not, and over the years wage withholding requirements have become increasingly constrictive.

As it presently stands, §§3401 and 3402 of the Code set the requirements for filing with one's employer Form W-4, the Employee's Withholding Allowance Certificate. The W-4 Form is used by the employee to instruct his employer as to how much money is to be withheld from his periodic pay for federal income tax purposes.

The W-4 Form as we know it today was created by changes to the tax law brought about by the Tax Reform Act of 1976. Prior to 1976, the W-4 was referred to as an Employee's Withholding Exemption Certificate. On the exemption certificate, you claimed only those exemptions to which you were entitled under §151 of the Code. Section 151 permits a deduction from gross income of $1,250 for each person whose support you pay at least 51% of during the course of the year. Additional exemptions are allowed for persons who are blind, or in excess of 65 years of age. These exemptions are claimed on the tax return, Form 1040, under the heading entitled "Exemptions."

According to the pre-1976 system, if you were married and had two children, the total number of exemptions you were entitled to claim on the 1040 would be four (one for yourself, one for your spouse, and one for each child.) Accordingly, four were all the exemptions you were entitled to claim on the W-4 for purposes of wage withholding.

Section 3402 has undergone much change since 1976, but the law as it presently stands allows one to claim, for purposes of withholding, any exemptions to which he would be entitled on the 1040 Form.[4] These are referred to as withholding "exemptions." In **addition** to the exemptions, he may claim additional reductions to withholding, referred to by §3402(m) as "allowances." Allowances are defined as anticipated itemized deductions, including anticipated tax credits to which one would be entitled to claim on the 1040 at the end of the year.

Existing law gives a person the right to adjust his withholding to match his tax liability. One major reason the law was changed in 1976 was that most citizens had a problem with over-withholding during the course of the year. What typically happened was that excess taxes were taken from the pay on a weekly basis, leaving the citizen in a weakened financial state year round. At the end of the year, when a tax return was filed, more times than not a large refund would be received. This placed a drain on the Treasury.

Now, legislation permits a citizen to take into consideration when setting his withholding status the itemized deductions and tax credits to which he will be entitled at the year's end. Consequently, where a person will itemize deductions to take advantage of such expenses as interest, medical expenses, and the like, or is entitled to a tax credit of one kind or another, it would behoove him to take these factors into consideration when preparing his Form W-4.

Under the present law, we are not limited, where withholding is concerned, to just dependents as we once were. The instructions to Form W-4 give full details as to how one can take advantage of the allowance system provided for in Code §3402(m). You should read them carefully.

QUESTION 147
If I expect to pay no taxes during the current year, must I submit to withholding?

This question arises as a natural outgrowth of the previous explanation. If a person is permitted to adjust his withholding to match his tax liability, and he reasonably estimates that his liability for a given year will be zero, must he then submit to wage withholding? The answer is found in §3402(n) of the Code. There we find a two-pronged test for determining

---
[4] See 26 USC §3402(f).

whether one may legally exempt himself from the withholding of federal income taxes.

The first prong is that one must have paid no income taxes for the previous year. If, in say 1985, you paid zero income taxes — that is to say not only were you not required to pay additional amounts at the end of the year but you received a **full refund** of all taxes paid in — then you meet the first requirement of the test. The second prong relates to the current year, which, in our example, would be 1986. If you anticipate paying zero income taxes in 1986 by reason of facts and circumstance known to you at the time of filing your Form W-4, then you would have met the second prong of the test.

Only after meeting **both** elements of the test can you exempt yourself from withholding. This is done by writing the word "exempt" on line three of Form W-4. Be mindful, however, that if either of the two prongs is not met, then you cannot legally exempt yourself from wage withholding.

QUESTION 148
Will the IRS ever see my W-4 Form?

Under regulations promulgated by the IRS in 1981, so-called "questionable Forms W-4" are forwarded to the IRS for review by the "W-4 coordinator." The job of the W-4 coordinator is to review all questionable Forms W-4 to determine whether they are proper. The regulations[5] require employers to forward to the IRS any Form W-4 which claims more than 14 withholding allowances, or on which a citizen has claimed to be exempt from withholding and earns $200 per week or more.

Once the W-4 is received, it will be reviewed for accuracy. The IRS will then mail to the citizen a letter stating that the form is under review, and will call for the completion of Form 6355, Worksheet to Determine Withholding Allowances. From the worksheet and your prior year's income tax return, the IRS will determine whether the W-4 is acceptable as filed.

If the IRS gets no response to the inquiry, the regulations allow them to instruct the employer to disregard the W-4 and to withhold income taxes as though the citizen were a single person claiming one withholding allowance. The result of

---

[5] The regulations are part of the Questionable Form W-4 Program, and were implemented under §3402 of the Code.

course, is that substantially more taxes are withheld than might otherwise be required.

In addition to the power to instruct the employer to disregard a W-4, the IRS has the authority under §6682 to assess a $500 penalty for filing a "false Form W-4." This penalty is an assessable penalty not subject to the deficiency procedures normally afforded a citizen in a monetary dispute with the IRS.[6]

After billing, if the penalty is not paid, it will be collected through levy on the citizen's wages or bank account. In addition, criminal penalties are provided for the filing of false withholding forms.[7]

QUESTION 149
Must I file a Form W-4?

Code §3402(j)(2) requires the filing of a Form W-4 "on or before the commencement of employment." However, there is no penalty for failure to file a form, other than that inferred in §3402, which calls for an employer to treat an employee as a single person claiming one allowance if no form is filed designating any different status.

QUESTION 150
Can I change my Form W-4 after it has been filed?

Section 3402 generally speaks to your obligation to change your Form W-4 at any time should your circumstances change. Therefore, if you've recently been married or had a child, you should change your W-4 to reflect that. Also, if you haven't been claiming allowances to which you are entitled, you'd be justified in amending the form to accommodate such a claim.

QUESTION 151
Must independent contractors file Form W-4?

A W-4 Form must be filed by "employees" as that terms is defined by §3401. A person who is a self-employed contractor need not file a Form W-4. For example, suppose you are a self-employed plumber. As such, you bid on plumbing jobs made available by general contractors. When successfully chosen as the plumbing contractor for a particular job, you then work for a specified sum, which is not subject to

---
[6] See Questions 46 and 86
[7] See Question 113.

withholding for federal income tax or Social Security tax purposes. You are paid in full by the general contractor. As a self-employed, however, you are expected to file quarterly estimates and make installment payments of your anticipated tax liability.

Recently, an addition to the law found at §3402(s) requires that the person making the payments secure from the person to whom the payments are to be made an accurate Social Security or Employer Identification number[8] for the purpose of reporting the payments on Form 1099[9]. If no number is on file, or if an inaccurate number is on file, the independent contractor will be subject to 20% withholding on the payments which are due him. The 20% withholding is the IRS' way of forcing everybody to associate a number with his name so that payments to him can be traced.

QUESTION 152
What's the difference between an independent contractor and an employee?

This question has been the subject of much litigation over the years. From the standpoint of the employer, it is cheaper to work through contractors than employees, since with employees go the obligations of wage withholding, and the payment of unemployment and Social Security taxes, not to mention all the record keeping that goes with those tax collection tasks. Independent contractors, since they are, in the strictest sense, self-employed, do not carry with them the burden of these payments. They are paid in full for their work and they are to assume the burden of accounting for and paying their own tax liability.

An understanding of the legal difference between the two begins with a look at the "employer." If the person for whom the work is **performed** has the right to direct the manner in which the work is performed, the time and place in which the work is to be done, provides tools and insurance for worker, and is the only party who stands to gain or lose from the job, then you have an employer-employee relationship. As the employer, you will be subjected to the tax and withholding requirements on your employees.

---

[8] The EIN is used by businesses in place of an SSN.
[9] Form 1099, Information Return is required to be filed under §6041 when payments in a single year exceed $600.

On the other hand, if the person who **performs** the work has the sole right to direct how the work will be done, can delegate the work to other persons, can direct the time and place in which the work is to be done, provides his own tools and insurance, and stands to gain or lose from the job, then a general contractor-independent contractor relationship exists. Under this arrangement, the general contractor is not subject to the employment taxes and withholding requirements created for and binding upon employees.

QUESTION 153
Why has my bank recently demanded my Social Security number?

Code §3451 was added by TEFRA and made payments of interest and dividends subject to federal withholding laws. Payments of this kind are subject to withholding at the rate of 10%. However, as pointed out above, if no accurate Social Security number is on file for the person to whom the money is due, then the person making the payments will be forced to withhold 20% of the amount due.

It is interesting to note that even though the law requires the number (lest 20% be withheld) only where payments are to be made, banks are routinely demanding the number under the color of this law for accounts through which no payments are to be made. For example, if you own a checking account which does not pay you interest, then the bank would have no right to demand a number under the authority of §3451. However, where you have a savings account paying passbook interest, the bank will demand the number or withhold 20% of your interest in the absence of it.

QUESTION 154
What kind of payments are subject to the new withholding law?

Code §3454 defines the areas subject to withholding under §3451. Three types of payments are included. They are interest, dividends, and patronage dividends. The law defines these terms as follows:

1. Interest means —
   a. interest on any obligation in registered form or of a type offered to the public;
   b. interest on deposits with persons carrying on the banking business;

c. any amount paid by a mutual savings bank, savings and loan association, building and loan association, cooperative bank, homestead association, credit union, industrial loan association or bank, or similar organization, in respect of deposits, investment certificates, or withdrawable or repurchaseable shares;

d. interest on amounts held by an insurance company under an agreement to pay interest thereon;

e. interest on deposits with brokers; and

f. interest paid on amounts held by investment companies and on amounts invested in other pooled funds or trusts.

2. Dividend means —

a. any distribution by a corporation which is a dividend as defined by Code §316; and

b. any payment made by a stockbroker to any person as a substitute for a dividend so defined.

3. Patronage dividend means —

a. the amount of a dividend paid by any organization which pays it patrons (such as a farmer's cooperative)[10]

As you can see, the law applies only where you are entitled to payments in any one of the three forms specified. Where you are not entitled to payments in any of these three forms, the organization holding your money has no right to withhold any percentage where you fail to provide a Social Security number.

QUESTION 155
Must I give my Social Security number to anyone who asks for it?

The Social Security number (SSN) is referred to by the IRS as a "Taxpayer Identification number." This is an anomaly because the Social Security Act provides that the number was never to used as a means of identification. In fact, your Social Security card states on its face that it is not an "identification" number or card. Still, at an ever increasing rate, the SSN is being associated with the holder as the "number of his name."

There have been cases in the past where persons have objected to giving their SSN to others on the grounds that it invades their right of privacy. There can be no doubt that once you have given your number in just a few instances, as in the

---

[10] Code §1388(a) contains a full definition of a patronage dividend.

case of opening a bank account, or filing a tax form, the number may well be irrevocably tied to your name.

Attacks on the number as being an invasion of the right of privacy have failed. Courts have taken the position that there is no right of privacy in one's name, and, hence, there is no right of privacy in the number to which it has become married.

An attack in a completely different vein, however, has borne fruit. The attack was launched by members of the Christian community who have taken the position that the SSN is or could be the "Mark of the Beast" talked of in the Scriptures.[11] This conclusion was reached after reflection upon the language of the Biblical author, which provides that the "Beast" causes all, "great and small, rich and poor, free and bond," to receive a mark. Going on, the author observes that no man might buy or sell unless he has that mark, which is identified as "the number of his name." In conclusion, Scripture states that anybody who receives the "Mark of the Beast" will not be entitled to reap the promise of eternal life.

If, as a Christian, you have concerns about the SSN consistent with the admonitions of Revelation 13, one federal court has provided relief. In **Stevens v. Berger**,[12] a federal district court ruled that where parents were religiously opposed to the use of the number, a number could not be forced upon the children of those parents. Moreover, the court held that where one refuses to accept or obtain a number on religious grounds, he could not be denied any rights to which he would otherwise have been entitled. To do so would be to discriminate on religious grounds, which is illegal.

In short, the only reason which appears to have substance in the law for refusing to obtain or use an SSN is the grounds of religious opposition. Of course, if you have asserted religious opposition to obtaining or using an SSN, you must reasonably and in good faith adhere to the basis underlying your objection. The law and good conscience would not permit jumping on the band wagon as a mere excuse to avoid what may be only an inconvenience.

QUESTION 156
Does the IRS require an SSN for tax filings?

As you probably know, the 1040 Form and nearly every other IRS form that comes to mind has a space for the SSN.

---

[11] See the New Testament Book of Revelation, Chapter 13:16-18.
[12] 428 F.Supp. 896 (N.Y. 1977).

Also, tax regulations "require" an SSN on all filings, and in fact, impose a $5 fine on the individual for failure to include his SSN. We have already discussed the perils of failure to use a number if you have interest-paying bank accounts.

If you have a religious objection to the use of the number, this objection could well be carried to the IRS. Your objection would have to be made at the time any attempt to levy the fine was made, and if necessary, you'd have to argue your case through the system as we have discussed in the previous Chapters.

QUESTION 157
If I don't have the money to pay my taxes, should I file the return without the money?

This question is one of the most asked questions about federal income tax procedure. Many people, in an effort to "do what's right," file the return when required, but without paying the money. The reason always given for this action is that while the money wasn't available, one believed it best to file the return anyway. The tax could always be paid later. What happens next is that the IRS almost immediately begins levying on banks and paychecks in order to collect the tax. In a state of dismay, the citizen mourns: "If only they'd given me just two months, I'd have been able to pay."

Understand that there are two ways in which a tax liability becomes assessed. The first is for the citizen to assess himself the tax by filing a return which declares an amount of money due and owing. This tax liability is recorded on the account of the individual, and becomes an assessment against him. The assessment is legally collectible by the IRS through enforced collection procedures. The other way is for the IRS to assert a deficiency, after which you must be afforded all of the administrative appeal rights within the IRS. Only after these remedies have been exhausted by you can the tax be assessed and legally collected.

Where a return is filed but the tax is not paid, it is no wonder that the IRS immediately begins collection with enforced action. It would be as though you went to the local car dealer, bought a new car and signed a contract stating that you owed the sum of $10,000 but didn't pay. That money, more likely than not, would be collectible by the car dealer though enforced action such as repossession of the car without much in the way of notice to you.

The act of signing a tax return which declares an amount due and owing is no different. You tell the IRS: "I owe you money but I'm not going to pay it just yet." You ask the IRS to be patient but the IRS has no patience in this regard. They will go after the money with all the collection tools available to them.

On the other hand, if no return is filed, you will be assessed the penalties for late filing and interest on the late payment. These penalties are discussed at Question 39. Based upon the information just given, you be the judge of whether a return should ever be filed without full payment of the tax at the time of filing the return.

QUESTION 158
Can I get an extension of time to pay the tax?

The only way an extension of time to pay can be arranged is through the Collection Division. We have discussed the intricacies of Collection in Chapter Three. Extensions of time can, however, be granted to file a return. Code §6081 allows the IRS to extend the period for filing a return for a "reasonable period" not to exceed 6 months.

An application for extension of time to file is submitted on Form 4868. This extension is automatic **if** the estimated tax for the year has been paid.[13] Note that the extension does not allow an extension to pay the tax, only to file the return. Consequently, if at the end of the year, but before the time for filing your tax return, it is apparent that you cannot get the return filed for some reason, Form 4868 can be filed. If you have been subjected to wage withholding during the course of the year which you reasonably believe will be sufficient to satisfy your tax liability, that can be stated on Form 4868.

Filing such a form will give you an automatic two-month extension of time to file the return. Once the return is prepared, if for some reason it shows an additional tax liability due, it should be paid at the time the return is filed. The submission of the application for extension will prevent any penalties for negligence and delinquency from being assessed.

---

[13] See Rev. Reg. §1.6081-4.

QUESTION 159
Is my tax return and its information confidential?

Code §6103 provides a measure of protection for tax returns and information in the possession of the government by reason of return filings. The problem is that there are so many exceptions to the statute that the term "confidentiality" is really a misnomer.

The law authorizes disclosure of your tax return and its information to Congress; members of the Joint Committee on Taxation; census personnel; any other federal law enforcement agency, such as the FBI, whether or not that agency is involved in administering the tax laws; state and local governments and government agencies for administering their tax laws; the Social Security Administration; the President of the United States. Virtually any federal or state agency which can claim an interest in the information contained in the return has access to it. Your tax information can even be disclosed to foreign governments with whom the United States has a tax treaty.

QUESTION 160
Who is the IRS?

Simply put, the Internal Revenue Service is the government agency charged with the duty of collecting federal tax revenues. The agency is responsible for the collection of not only personal and corporate income taxes, but it collects federal excise taxes on such things as tires, alcohol, cigarettes, etc. The collection of Social Security and self-employment taxes has also been appointed to the IRS. In short, every tax imaginable in existence at the federal level is collected by the Internal Revenue Service.

The IRS will also assist the various state govenrments in the collection of their state income taxes. Nearly every state which has an income tax has an information reciprocity agreement with the IRS. That is, the IRS will supply the particular state with collection information and the state will supply the IRS with such information.

An agreement of this kind exists not only with domestic states, but with foreign nations as well. The United States has entered into tax treaties with several foreign nations. These treaties are designed to facilitate international tax collection. To the extent that the United States is a party with any other country in a tax treaty, information about your income and expenses could be shared with that foreign body.

QUESTION 161
When did the IRS come into existence?
The Internal Revenue Service, known then as the Bureau of Internal Revenue, came into existence in 1913 with the ratification of the 16th Amendment,[14] the so-called income tax amendment. Prior to 1913, the United States did not have an income tax for any appreciable amount of time. The first income tax act on the books was struck down in 1894 by the Supreme Court as unconstitutional.[15]

In 1909, Congress passed the Corporation Excise Tax Act, which was the forerunner to the Income Tax Act. Much legal dispute and, consequently, much legal authority was generated as a result of the Corporation Excise Tax Act of 1909. To a large degree, this legal authority has carried over into the Income Tax Act when that law became effective after 1913.

In 1926, another massive income tax law was passed which changed, among other things, the name of the agency from Bureau of Internal Revenue to the Internal Revenue Service. Since then, several mountainous changes to the tax laws have taken place, but in the recent past Congress seems to be especially ambitious where changes to the tax laws are concerned.

Since 1976, with the passage of the Tax Reform Act of 1976, the Economic Recovery Tax Act of 1980, the Tax Equity and Fiscal Responsibility Act of 1982, and the 1984 Tax Reform Act, four major Congressional rewrites have overhauled nearly every aspect of our federal tax system. This, of course, says nothing of the Reagan Tax proposal, which, at the time of this writing, has not been accepted into law. This latest proposal threatens to again completely revamp our entire tax system.

Through all of this writing and rewriting, the one thing which remains constant is the IRS' power to collect taxes. With all the talk of budget cuts and belt-tightening that catapulted President Reagan into office in 1980, the one

---

[14] Whether the 16th Amendment was ever legally ratified is currently the subject of heated litigation in the federal courts at various levels across the United States. Research has shown that records evidencing individual state ratification of the amendment may have been falsified. The question now before the federal courts is whether the 16th Amendment is a product of a fraudulent undertaking.
[15] **Pollack v. Farmer's Loan and Trust**, 158 U.S. 601 (1895).

agency which saw its manpower **increased** was the IRS. Shortly after taking office, Reagan authorized the hiring of 5000 additional Revenue Agents. In addition, as we have learned from the Plan, the IRS has spent nearly $100 million upgrading their computer systems nationwide. All of this — ostensibly — to aid the collection of income taxes.

QUESTION 162
How is the IRS organized?

The Internal Revenue Service, as a federal agency, is under the authority of the Commissioner of Internal Revenue. The Commissioner is immediately answerable to the Secretary of Treasury, which, of course, is a Cabinet post. The Commissioner is responsible for the overall operation of the IRS. The National Office of the IRS is made up of nine primary branches. These branches are headed by an Assistant Commissioner in eight cases, and by a Chief Counsel in the ninth case. The nine branches are:

1. Taxpayer Service and Returns Processing,
2. Resources Management,
3. Compliance,
4. Data Services,
5. Employee Plans and Exempt Organizations,
6. Inspection,
7. Planning and Research,
8. Technical, and
9. Legal.

A brief explanation of each division and its function follows:

1. Taxpayer Service. This branch handles all incoming tax returns and processing of the same. That includes instilling tax information into computers and doling out refunds. They also administer taxpayer assistance programs and advisory services.

2. Resources Management. This branch trains IRS employees, and, as the name suggests, generally controls all of the facilities, including money and personnel, entrusted to the IRS.

3. Compliance. This is the one branch of the IRS with which members of the general public will most likely come in contact. They handle audits, investigations, appeals by taxpayers of internal decisions, and collection of delinquent taxes.

4. Data Services. Data Services is responsible for the development and maintenance of all IRS computer systems nationwide.

5. Employee Plans and Exempt Organizations. This is where the IRS controls our country's exempt organizations, such as churchs and charities, and employee retirement plans, such as 401(k) plans.

6. Inspection. The Inspection branch is internal in nature. They conduct internal audits and handle internal security. They have no contact with the general public.

7. Planning and Research. This branch prepares and circulates internal managment documents and memos, and assists in researching and analyzing general operations procedures. They also do legislative research. They wrote the Strategic Plan.

8. Technical. All of the tax forms and publications used for federal tax purposes are generated by the Technical branch.

9. Legal. The last branch is the Legal branch. This section is made up of the lawyers who represent the IRS when it finds itself in Tax Court or in need of legal advice.

Under the authority of the National Office and the Commissioner of Internal Revenue, we find the Field Offices. The Field Offices are made up of seven regions, each headed by a Regional Commissioner answerable to the Commissioner. Each region is further broken down into districts, and each district is headed by a District Director who is answerable to the Regional Commissioner. In most cases, a district consists of a single state. The seven regions are organized geographically as follows:

1. Western Region: Alaska, Hawaii, California (broken into two districts), Washington, Oregon, Idaho, Nevada, Arizona, Utah, Montana.

2. Southwest Region: Wyoming, Colorado, Kansas, New Mexico, Oklahoma, Arkansas, Texas (broken into two districts), Louisiana.

3. Midwest Region: North Dakota, South Dakota, Nebraska, Minnesota, Iowa, Missouri, Wisconsin, Illinois (broken into two districts).

4. Central Region: Michigan, Indiana, Kentucky, Ohio (broken into two districts), West Virginia.

5. Southwest Region: Tennessee, North Carolina, South Carolina, Mississippi, Alabama, Georgia, Florida.

6. Mid-Atlantic Region: Pennsylvania (broken into two districts), New Jersey, Virginia, Maryland, Delaware, Washington, D.C., Puerto Rico, Virgin Islands.

7. North-Atlantic Region: New York (broken into two districts), New Hampshire, Maine, Vermont, Massachusetts, Conneticutt, Providence Rhode Island.

As pointed out earlier, the one branch with which a citizen is most likely to come into direct contact is the Compliance branch. The Compliance branch is broken into five divisions, each of which is responsible for direct taxpayer contact. We have given attention to four of these divisions in this book. The five divisions are:

1. Examination. This division is the one which conducts all audits of income tax returns. Persons employed in this division are called Revenue Agents.

2. Appeals. This division handles taxpayer appeals of disputed Revenue Agent decisions made in connection with an audit. Persons employed in the Appeals Division are called Appeals Officers.

3. Collection. This division is made up of Revenue Officers whose duty it is to collect unpaid federal taxes. Think of this division as the federal collection agency. Revenue Officers are the IRS employees who make seizures of property, such as bank accounts, automobiles and paychecks to settle unpaid tax depts.

4. Criminal Investigation. This division handles the cloak and dagger type investigations of taxpayers suspected of criminal activity. Employees here are called Special Agents, and they gather the evidence which is ultimately used in the prosecution of taxpayers for any of the several criminal violations enumerated in the tax code.

5. Office of International Operations. This office coordinates with foreign countries in the enforcement of international tax treaties.

This brief statement is not intended to constitute an exhaustive analysis of IRS organization. It would take pages and pages of boring discourse to fully explain their structure. The above is intended merely as an overview which will make further research, if desired, somewhat easier.

Chapter Six
WHITHER AMERICA?
The Ultimate Question

QUESTION 163
What is "The Law"?

Since childhood we've been taught that "ours is a nation of laws, not men." We've heard that "no man is above the law." We've learned that "we all must obey the law," and that "ignorance of the law is no excuse."

What we haven't been taught is this: What is the law that we are supposed to obey?; which law is ignorance no excuse?; and which law is no man above? We know that Congress and the various state legislatures spend months each year passing laws into existence, and the previous five chapters have been dedicated to discussing the law as it's presented in the Internal Revenue Code. But is that the law to which these worn-out cliche's refer?

I think not.

When our nation was founded, a blueprint for government was drawn by our early statesmen. This document became the pattern by which our officials were to govern their actions. The blueprint is the Constitution of the United States. The Constitution heralds itself as the "Supreme Law of the Land,[1] and it has been recognized and held that any Congressional enactment which is repugnant to the Constitution is without force and effect.

The Constitution makes provisions for the operation of our government, from the conduct of the Congress and its authority to the President of the United States and his authority. Our courts are created and specific power and authority is delegated to them. The Constitution provides for the manner in which our various Congressmen are to be elected, the fashion in which they will enact laws and manner in which the government is to be financed. In short, every contingency has been provided for.

Not only have the rights and powers of the government been set forth in the Constitution in detail, but the limitations of the government have also been delineated. Our founding fathers had expressly provided for those areas in which the

---
[1] Constitution, Article VI.

government was, under no conditions, to tread. The Bill of Rights, adopted as part of the Constitution in the form of the first 10 Amendments, establishes the rights of the people, expressly limiting the power of government. Thus, the Constitution should be seen as a limitation on the power of the government, and a guarantee to the people of all natural rights.

A look at the pre-Constitution era sentiment of leading world figures will help us to understand why the Constitution was written in the way it was. The establishment of a Constitutional government of limited powers was an act unknown in the world at the time of its adoption in 1787. Several years earlier, in 1776, the newly formed Colonial government shocked the world with its Declaration of Independence from England.

What was shocking was not so much that independence had been declared, for that act had taken place numerous times before in history. The shock came upon reading the Declaration of Independence, penned by Thomas Jefferson. In it, Jefferson stated that governments derive "their just power from the consent of the governed..." This language for the first time manifested in clearly written, easily understood language an idea first popularized by a Puritan Minister named Samual Rutherford.

Rutherford, in his book **Lex Rex, or The Law and the Prince**, blasted the theory of "the divine right of Kings," much touted by European monarchs. The theory held that Kings were empowered by divine intervention, and hence had absolute authority to create whatever law they deemed necessary to preserve the Crown. Jefferson, in keeping with the attitude of Rutherford and others, maintained that it was the people who ordained governments, and in that context government was established only to serve and protect the people.

The Declaration of Independence observes that whenever a government becomes destructive of those ends, it is:

> "the Right of the People to to alter or to abolish it, and to institute new Government, laying its foundation on such principles and organizing its powers in such form, as to them shall seem more likely to effect their Safety and Happiness."

Jefferson was not alone in his position that government was a creation of the people installed only to protect their life, liberty and property. At and before the time of Congress' Declaration of Independence from England, Alexander Hamilton wrote much in an effort to justify the act of severance from the authority of the Crown.

Drawing from Blackstone, the great English jurist, Hamilton observed that the relationship between civil government and the people "must be a voluntary compact" and that civil government was responsible to secure the "absolute rights" of the people. He also opined that no "man had any moral power to deprive another of his life, limbs, property or liberty, nor had the least authority" to command or exact obedience from him.[2]

Grounded in the sound observations of not only the preacher Rutherford and the professor Blackstone, but upon the lawyer John Locke, and the philosopher Thomas Paine, our Colonial forefathers forged the United States of America. At its foundation was the Constitution. It was and is the first chart for a society wherein the people were vested with the absolute rights to life, liberty and property, and where the government was instituted by them for the sole and express purpose of preserving those rights.

I would define an absolute right as one which cannot be liened, impinged, or hindered in any way, without the consent of the individual. Therefore, unless upon conviction of violating another's absolute rights, government cannot constrain the exercise of absolute rights for any reason, however "necessary" or benevolent the stated purpose. An early Supreme Court decision has delineated some of the specific rights absolutely protected under the Constitution. In **Meyer v. Nebraska**,[3] Mr. Justice McReynolds, speaking for the Court, said:

> "Without doubt, (liberty) denotes not merely freedom from bodily restraint, but also the right of the individual to contract, to engage in any of the common occupations of life, to acquire useful knowledge, to marry, establish a home and bring up children, to worship God according to

---

[2] See Hamilton's **A Full Vindication of the Measures of the Congress from the Calumnies of their Enemies**, (1774); and **A Farmer Refuted: Or, A More Impartial and Comprehensive View of the Dispute between Great Britain and the Colonies, Intended as a Further Vindication of the Congress**, (1775).
[3] 262 U.S. 390 (1923).

the dictates of his own conscience, and, generally, to enjoy those privileges long recognized at common law as essential to the orderly pursuit of happiness by free men.''

By establishing a Constitutional government, a role reversal had taken place. No longer would the people exist for the benefit of the state as they had in England for centuries. Rather, the Constitution was to ensure that the state would exist only for the protection of the absolute rights of the people.

The Constitution, then, is the law of land to which the earlier cliches apply. It is the Constitution which all government officials are sworn to uphold, and it is the Constitution which forms the basis of power for all government actions in this country. Any action taken by any government official which is not in strict conformance with the dictates of the Constitution must be said to be void and without effect. Similarly, any action which violates the rights of the individual must be said to be void and without effect.

Does the taking of one's property by the government without his consent constitute a violation of absolute rights? Where the purpose is taxation to "support the government," does the government have the power to set aside absolute rights because of the "necessity of running the government"?

A statement on this very subject was made in the Magna Carta, the English document of freedom signed in 1215 A.D. It held that the King's men could not enter upon a man's private property to take even his firewood "without his consent." Is the taking of one's wages without his consent a violation of these long-established principles of absolute property rights?

In the early years of our nation's history, the courts — especially the Supreme Court — were vigilant in protecting the absolute rights of the people as memorialized in the Constitution. Intrusions of the rights of the people were not permitted, regardless of the cause. Any governmental action which infringed upon an inalienable right was condemned and forbidden. The Constitution was read in a light most favorable to the people, not the government.

Where the courts found that a provision was not as clear as it might be in a given factual situation, the ambiguity was to be resolved in favor of the individual. Also, where government action directly implicated the rights of the citizens, the government was to be promptly chased back within its Constitutional boundaries.

This kind of "strict interpretation" of the Constitution was called for by both Jefferson and Hamilton. Hamilton spoke most loudly on the subject of strict adherence to the language of the document. He said:

> "If we set out with justice, moderation, liberality, and a scrupulous regard to the Constitution, the government will acquire a spirit and tone productive of permanent blessings to the community. If, on the contrary, the public councils are guided by humor, passion, and prejudice; or from resentment to individuals, or a dread of partial inconveniences, the Constitution is slighted, or explained away, upon every frivolous pretext, the future spirit of government will be feeble, distracted and arbitrary. The rights of the subjects will be the sport of every party vicissitude. There will be no settled rule of conduct, but every thing will fluctuate with the alternate prevalency of contending factions.[4]

The message of this letter is brief; continuity of the moral fabric of society is dependent upon legal absolutes, especially where the rights of citizens are concerned. If the government is free to "explain away" the protections of the Constitution, in the end there will be no Constitution. If the rights of the citizens are made the "sport" of every governmental opinion change, in the end there will be no rights of the citizens.

Hamilton's fear and the malady against which he so earnestly cautioned — Constitutional interpretation — has inflicted our nation in a most violent fashion. The Supreme Court, taking its lead from Justice Felix Frankfurter, now asserts the position that the "Constitution is what the Court says it is," and that those interpretations are, rather than the Constitution itself, the "Supreme law of the land.[5]

The aftermath of several years of interpretation of the Constitution by Supreme Court Justices is the very result feared by Hamilton and Jefferson. One by one, the rights

---

[4] Hamilton's second letter to the Considerate Citizens of New-York Containing Remarks on Mentor's Reply. (1784).
[5] See **Cooper v. Aaron**, 358 U.S. 1 (1958).

expressly preserved to the people have been eroded by decades of judicial backwash. The most recent statements by the Supreme Court in a case involving substantial Constitutional rights affords a more than adequate example.

On February 28, 1984, the Supreme Court delivered its opinion in **United States v. Doe**.[6] There, the Court addressed the question of whether the government could force an individual to produce his private books and records in the face of a Fifth Amendment claim against self-incrimination.

The state of the law prior to **Doe** was quite settled. The well-traveled path was hacked out by the Court nearly 100 years previous to **Doe**. In the 1886 decision of **Boyd v. United States**,[7] the Supreme Court held that the Fifth Amendment created a "zone of privacy" which protects an individual and his personal records from compelled production. In short, the government could not force a person to produce his personal books and records any more than they could force him to give testimony against himself.

Literally hundreds of court decisions had followed the **Boyd** logic to where, by the time **Doe** was presented to the Supreme Court, a legion of well-grounded case authority weighed against the idea that the government could force a person to open his private books and papers.

In **Doe**, however, the Supreme Court "sounded the death-knell" for **Boyd** and held that a person had no right to privacy where his personal books and records were concerned. To quote Justice O'Connor in her concurring opinion, "The Fifth Amendment provides absolutely no protection for the contents of private papers of any kind."

With the stroke of a judicial pen, your right to privacy in you personal records — a right in existence since the beginning of our country — has been destroyed. As it presently stands, the law permits any governmental agency to force you to deliver your private papers and records for whatever reason they deem them necessary. Once delivered, they can be used against you in whatever way the agency deems appropriate.

The rationale used in arriving at the decision is even more offensive to reason than the decision itself. Justice Powell rendered the opinion of the Court, and in it observed that the

---

[6] 104 S.Ct. 1237 (1984).
[7] 116 U.S. 616 (1886).

Fifth Amendment protects a person only from "compelled incriminations," i.e., statements which he is forced to make.

Going on, he pointed out that since one is not **forced** to prepare private papers or documents, the protections of the Fifth Amendment do not extend to those papers. In other words, since you voluntarily prepared your private papers, you can be forced to turn them over to government agencies.

What the Justice's sophomoric logic has overlooked is that it is the act of transmitting information from a private party to the government agency which is protected. Whether a person has or has not voluntarily prepared that information is not the issue. The question is whether or not he is forced to transmit data to government authorities. This, the Fifth Amendment says, he cannot be forced to do.

The Fifth Amendment states that no person shall be compelled to "be a witness against himself." That is to say, one can't be forced to give information about himself to any government agency. To say that forced transmittal of private papers to a government agency does not violate the Fifth Amendment because one voluntarily prepared the papers strains the limits of reason and common sense.

The Supreme Court has been rendering decisions which undercut the integrity of the Constitution with alarming rapidity. The Supreme Court seems to have lost sight of the fact that they, as members of the federal judiciary, have taken oaths to uphold and defend the Constitution from all enemies, foreign and domestic. Ironically, the very court which our founding fathers created as the mainstay of Constitutional safeguards has itself become the chief adversary to Constitutional principles.

The Constitution guarantees every citizen a republican form of government.[8] Throughout the 20th Century, citizens and government authorities alike have taken kindly to referring to this country as a "democracy." Such an appellation is erroneous.

By Constitutional requirement, the United States is a republic. A republican system of government is one based upon a fixed standard of law. Hence, the oft-used expression: "We are a nation of law and not of men." Under a republic, every citizen — as well as the government itself — is subject

---

[8] Constitution, Article IV.

to a higher law which forms a rigid standard of right and wrong. What is unjust for the government one year will continue to be unjust next year and the year after; likewise with the people. This is exactly the kind of standard Hamilton insisted upon.

In the United States, the Constitution is that higher law. Regardless of what the Congress or any government agency has to say on a particular subject, the Constitution is the final authority. And where the dictates of the lesser authority conflict with that of the higher authority, the higher authority prevails. The **only** role the courts of this country have is to lay the acts of Congress next to the plain language of the Constitution and decide whether the former squares with the latter. If not, it is the acts of Congress, not the Constitution, which must fall.

In a democracy, the majority rules through the imposition of "public opinion." Consequently, which ever way the winds of passion blow on a particular issue, that's the way in which the governmental authorities direct their action. As a result, the standard of right and wrong in society is subject to the ebb and flow of current special interests. Moreover, the government is seldom responsive to the "winds of public opinion," even if they are constant.

For example, when Ronald Reagan was elected to the Presidency in 1980, the main reasons for his success were his redundant promises to lower taxes and balance the federal budget. The overwhelming number of people who voted for Reagan sent the message loud and clear that "public opinion" demanded a tax break and a balanced federal budget. What Reagan actually did upon taking power was quite the opposite of what he said he would do.

In 1982, with the passage of the Tax Equity and Fiscal Responsibility Act (TEFRA) came the largest single increase in federal taxes in the history of the United States. Cleverly disguised as excise taxes[9] rather than easily detected income taxes, the American people were by and large unaware that their tax burden would be increased by some $98.3 billion over the subsequent several years. I don't have to tell you what the state of the federal budget is.

---

[9] An excise tax is a uniform tax upon a specific item. An example would be federal liquor and gasoline taxes. Every person pays the same rate of tax when purchasing an item carrying such a tax. The tax is increased only when the amount of a purchase is increased. Excise taxes were expressly provided for in our Constitution (Article 1, Sect. 8) and appear far more equitable than an income tax.

Democratic forms of government — responsive only to whimsical turns of popular opinion — do not respect the individual or his rights. The democratic form of government has as the focal point of its concern the interests of the government in promoting its policies. Always under the heading "for the public good," democratic forms of government impinge the rights of the individual to the point where people become mere tools of the state in carrying out its policies.

James Madison, in **The Federalist** No. 10[10] elucidated why our forefathers opted to form a republic, not a democracy. Madison contrasted the republic with the democracy, in a historical context, and drew this conclusion:

> "From this view of the subject it may be concluded that a pure democracy, by which I mean a society consisting of a small number of citizens, who assemble and administer the government in person, can admit of no cure for the mischiefs of faction. A common passion or interest will, in almost every case, be felt by a majority of the whole; a communication and concert result from the form of government itself; and there is nothing to check the inducements to sacrifice the weaker party or an obnoxious individual. Hence it is that such democracies have ever been spectacles of turbulence and contention; have ever been found incompatible with personal security or the rights of property; and have in general been as short in their lives as they have been violent in their deaths."

The role of government that Jefferson and Hamilton envisioned when the Constitution was drafted is, in a democracy, completely reversed, taking on the form of "Lord" rather than that of mere protector.

A long, steady pattern of transforming government from that of protector to that of "Lord" has finally culminated in vesting absolute authority in the hands of the state, leaving the citizen at the mercy of its claimed benevolence. This startling metamorphosis manifests itself in a recent Supreme Court decision.

---

[10] **The Federalist** were a series of 85 essays written by James Madison, Alexander Hamilton and John Jay. They appeared in New York newspapers from October 1787 to April 1788, under the pseudonym "Publius." The idea of the papers was conceived by Hamilton and they were calculated to fully explain the Constitution in an effort to overcome resistance to its ratification which some states presented.

In **United States v. Lee**,[11] the court has unceremoniously stamped out the last vestige of any claim to individual liberty by citizens in this country. As hard as that is to believe and accept, the Supreme Court has, in so many words, declared that individual rights must yield to the state when "an overriding governmental interest" is shown.

What the high Court said specifically is that any time the government can justify a need, it can impinge and nullify the religious, or presumably, any other liberty in which the individual is vested.

The **Lee** case involved a member of the Old Order Amish, who was a self-employed farmer and carpenter employing several persons. Because the Amish are religiously opposed to the kind of benefits offered by Social Security, Lee did not withhold or pay in either the employee's share or the employer's share of the required SS "contributions." He was assessed several thousand dollars by the IRS and, after paying a portion of the tax, (see Question 102) sued for a refund. After initial success, Lee found himself before the Supreme Court.

In its opinion, the Supreme Court specifically found that because of the Amish faith, "compulsory participation in the social security system interferes with (Lee's) Free Exercise[12] rights." But the Court justified direct interference by claiming that the government's "overriding interest" in collecting taxes permitted the violation.

In reaching its conclusion, the Court stated that "mandatory participation is indispensable to the fiscal vitality of the social security system." Pointing to a recent Congressional study on the financial soundness of the system, Chief Justice Berger observed that "Widespread individual voluntary coverage under social security. . .would undermine the soundness of the social security program."[13]

In no uncertain terms, the Court has said that because "we need the money," it is permissible to violate the Constitutional rights of citizens in order to get it. Thus, the only "overriding governmental interest" involved here is financial. To allow the Amish their absolute right to religion under the First

---
[11] 102 S.Ct. 1051 (1982).
[12] Referring to the right of free exercise of religion under the First Amendment.
[13] The Justice was citing Senate Report No. 404, 89th Congress, 1st Sess. Pt. III, U.S.Code Cong. & Admin. News (1965) pp. 1943, 2056.

Amendment threatens the program's image of fiscal soundness. Therefore, they cannot be afforded their rights any longer.

It is important to note that Lee and his religious brethern demanded nothing from the system in the first place. They had a program established and in place which provided for the needs of their families as well or better than the government program proposed to do. If a system does not permit the choice of particpation, is it sound at all?

In concluding, Justice Berger reasoned that religious beliefs "can be accommodated, but there is a point at which accommodation would radically restrict the operating latitude of the legislature." Allow me to translate that statement. The Justice said that the legislature must have free rein — total freedom — in passing laws. He has said that religious, and presumably all other rights, cannot be permitted to exist when they threaten the government's ability to unilaterally pass laws.

Have you read the Bill of Rights lately? Evidently Justice Berger has not. From beginning to end, the document places express restrictions upon the government's ability to pass laws. The First Amendment states in part:

> **Congress shall make no law** respecting an establishment of religion, **or prohibiting the free exercise thereof**. . .
> (Emphasis added.)

These restrictions directly and simply forbid the invasion of individual rights, yet the Chief Justice has held that all limitations are to be placed upon the **individual**, not upon **government**. The Chief Justice has said that the government must have absolute authority to pass any law it deems appropriate so long as an "overriding governmental interest" is shown, and that when an interest — such as "we need the money" — is demonstrated, then the individual's rights will no longer be "accommodated."

In **United States v. Lee** we see the result of a slow, steady process of government encroachment upon the liberties of the individual. Where our nation began as one in which the citizen was free of governmental intrusion into his private affairs, it has been, by judicial edict, transformed into just another police state with absolute authority vested in the hands of the government.

Our entire system of government has been changed right before our eyes. Oh, it's true that the democratic attributes our nation always had are still in place. We continue to vote for our representatives in Washington and at the State level, but the one meaningful attribute — the guarantee of a republican form of government and the assurance of liberty that goes with it — has been washed away in the sediment of judicial interpretation.

The most important portion of our Constitution, apart from the Bill of Rights, is the provision that every person in the United States is guaranteed a republican form of government. This is important because only under a republican system is a higher law recognized. Democracies do not recognize any higher law. They yield only to the whim of the moment.

At this point in our history, our federal government is determined to tax the American people to the breaking point in order to alleviate the problems brought on by uncontrolled government spending. In order to carry forth these efforts, the rights of the citizen must yield. The application of the higher law is suspended.

The one thing our founding fathers had in common, and the one thing which rings loudly throughout most early American writings, was the universal belief in a higher authority, and, hence, a higher law. They recognized and accepted the premise that the establishment of all civil government is based upon either of two basic religious beliefs.

The first is the humanist belief that man is autonomous. They knew that when a government is founded upon this premise, then such government will claim the absolute authority to arbitrarily direct the actions and the conscience of others in society.

It was this very belief, espoused by King George III, which triggered the American War for Independence. Unbeknown to most Americans, the Colonial struggle with England was not brought on by taxes. It was the King's edict of February 24, 1766, which drove the final nail in England's coffin of despotism. The edict held that the King had the "full power and authority to make laws and statutes of sufficient force and validity to bind the colonies and people of America, subjects of the Crown of Great Britain, in all cases whatsoever."

This example of governmental usurpation sent the emotions of freedom soaring in the hearts of our Colonial leaders, particularly Thomas Paine. And it was primarily Paine's writings, beginning with a brilliant fulmination against the King's edict and the theory of the divine right of Kings, which provided the intellectual justification for the drive to independence. The pamphlet **Common Sense** was issued on January 10, 1776. It was the philosophical heart and soul of the Revolutionary movement. Speaking of the edict in his next masterful work, **American Crisis I**, Paine said that "so unlimited a power could only belong to God."[14]

Conversely, the second premise recognizes that where government is established upon the Christian principles of a higher law and individual responsibility, then civil authority must and will be deprived of the power to direct in any way the conscience and actions of others. Christian law does not seek to impose arbitrary edicts and restrictions upon others. Christian law does, however, prevent one man from harming another's life, liberty and property unless for conviction of crime after due process has been afforded.

The whimsical tendency of man to change the law and provide criminal penalties for offenses not involving damage to another's life, liberty or property is absent from the Christian standard of authority. As a result, it is only in a Christian society where all people, including non-Christians, can live in peace without fear of government intrusion into their private affairs.

Even before the War for Independence, our early leaders were determined to establish a government based upon recognition that we are all subject to that higher law. In **Common Sense**, Paine called for the creation of a republic, similar to that which existed in "Old Testament Biblical times."

Jefferson insisted that because man was not capable of justly exercising absolute power over other men, governmental power

---

[14]Crisis I was written by the light of a campfire in late 1776. At that time, Paine was with General Washington's troops in New Jersey.

must be sparingly delegated and clearly specified in written form — the Constitution. Jefferson's words were: "Let no more be heard of confidence in man, but bind him down from mischief by the chains of the Constitution." The ultimate authority must alway rest with the people.

You ask, "How can the respect of the higher law — the Constitution — be restored?" Jefferson said, "If a nation expects to be ignorant and free it expects something that cannot be." The solution, then, begins with education. If each person in society knows and understands the limits of government, the government can more effectively be held within the bounds of those limits. On the other hand, where citizens are ignorant of the power of their government, if they believe that government is **vested** with absolute power, then that government will **exercise** absolute power.

The second and equally important step is to hold government accountable for violations of individual rights. Again I caution against joining the crusade of "movements." It is not necessary to join any "movement" to see that your own rights are enforced. If you understand what your rights are, then you know when those rights have been affronted by renegade government. You must take the offensive in the courts when that happens.

My experience with the law has shown clearly that he who controls the law controls the power and direction of government. The reason that government has been able to get away with the wholesale violation of rights **ala Lee** is because we have been taught that our participation in the affairs of government is limited to voting. We have been convinced that we are not to involve ourselves in the legal process where govenrment is concerned. As a result, our rights have been lost through default.

The courts have been provided us by our founding fathers as a means of redressing our grievances with government. The First Amendment guarantees this right. Through the dual process of education and judicial activism, the courts can be used as a means to bring pressure to bear on unjust government — to bring it in line with Constitutional limitations. We have to take back what is rightfully ours —

that which has been taken through a long process of unconstitutional judicial interpretation.

This is not so impossible as it seems. For years WINNING Seminars has been teaching people to use the court system to accomplish this very goal. Our seminar, **Understanding Taxes and Court Procedure**, has been taught to thousands of people all over the United States. Armed with knowledge learned in the seminar, citizens in every walk of life have enforced their claim to the American heritage — freedom and independence.

Our seminar is probably responsible for accomplishing more to benefit the Constitution than any other like-minded approach. Our students have used the material they've learned at both state and federal court levels to challenge unjust legal principles. In 14 Sections, we teach you everything from legal research to hiring a good lawyer. We teach you how to prosecute a suit to quash an IRS bank summons, and how to defend a summons enforcement proceeding for your personal books and records. We teach you how to prosecute a Tax Court petition, and how to defend against an unlawful seizure of your property. In over 400 pages of text material and eight 90-minute cassette tapes, you'll learn all of the detailed steps necessary to file a claim for refund, and a suit for refund. **Understanding Taxes and Court Procedure** shows you exactly how to take action to enforce your rights.

Only by taking affirmative action to educate yourself and to enforce your claims to freedom can we effect positive change from a Constitutional perspective. We have seen that the tendency of government is not to enforce the protections of liberty, but rather to erode them. That they have been successful in doing so is accounted for by the fact that the vast majority of Americans have no idea what is going on in our courts today. People are convinced that only criminals go to court. Consequently, they stay away. But criminals don't **go** to court, they are **taken** to court. Honest citizens **go** to court to enforce the rights to which they are lawfully entitled under the Constitution.

If you cannot or will not take action to control the direction of the law, you will not be able to control the direction of your government no matter how or where you exercise your right to vote. The election of President Reagan has proven, if there were any question beforehand, that elected officials are absolutely non-responsive to the desires of the people. They say what must be said to get elected, and the people hear the rhetoric only because it is rammed down their throats by the electronic media. After the election, people have no idea what their "representatives" in Congress or at the State level have done to protect their liberties. Chances are that they have done nothing.

Only through carefully orchestrated assults on unlawful government action through the court process, coupled with concentrated educational programs, can the power and direction of government be controlled. You are a citizen of this country. You have a responsibility to yourself, your children and God to see that a legacy of freedom is left to your progeny.

What are you going to do about it?

TABLE OF ABBREVIATIONS

"Cir." — When used in a case citation, refers to the stated circuit court of appeals, i.e., 8th Cir.

"Code" — Refers to the Internal Revenue Code of 1954, as amended.

"F.2d" — When used in a case citation, refers to the Federal Reporter, Second Series, published by West Publishing Co., St. Paul, MN.

"F.Supp." — When used in a case citation, refers to the Federal Supplement, published by West Publishing Co., St. Paul, MN.

"IRM" — Refers to the Internal Revenue Manual.

"MT" — Refers to an IR Manual Transmittal.

"Rev. Reg." — Refers to a Revenue Regulation.

"S.Ct." — When used in a case citation, refers to The Supreme Court Reporter, published by West Publishing Co., St. Paul, MN.

"U.S." — When used in a case citation, refers to the United States Supreme Court Reports, published by the U.S. Government Printing Office.

"U.S.C." — Refers to the United States Code, at the stated title and section, i.e., 18 U.S.C. §3161.

"U.S.T.C." — When used in a case citation, refers to the United States Tax Cases, published by Commerce Clearing House, Chicago, IL.

BIBLIOGRAPHY

Bastiat, Frederic, *The Law*, (1850), The Foundation for Economic Education, New York, 1977

Brant, Irving, *The Bill of Rights, Its Origin and Meaning*, Mentor Publishing, New York, 1967

Church, Frank, *Hearings before the Select Committee to Study Governmental Operations with respect to Intelligence Activities of the U.S.*, Ninety-fourth Congress, 1st Session, 3 Vol., (transcript) U.S. Government Printing Office, Washington, D.C., 1975

Congressional Research Service, *The Constitution of the United States of America, Analysis and Interpretation*, U.S. Government Printing Office, Washington, D.C., 1973

Foner, Philip S., *The Life and Major Writings of Thomas Paine*, Citadel Press, Secaucus, NJ, 1948

Hall, Verna M., *The Christian History of the Constitution*, The Foundation for American Christian Education, San Francisco, 1966

Larson, Martin A., *The Essence of Jefferson*, Joseph J. Binns, New York, 1977

Locke, John, (1632-1704) *An Essay Concerning Human Understanding*, 2 Vol., F.M. Rent and Sons, Ltd., London, 1961

Madison, James, *The Federalist*, with John Jay and Alexander Hamilton, (1787), M.W. Dunne, London, 1901

Malone, Dumas, *Jefferson and the Rights of Man*, Little Brown and Company Limited, 1951

_____, *Jefferson and the Ordeal of Liberty*, Little Brown and Company Limited, 1962

Morris, Richard B., *The Basic Ideas of Alexander Hamilton*, Pocket Books, Inc., New York, 1957

Rutherford, Rev. Samual, *Lex, Rex, or the Law and the Prince*, (1644), Sprinkle Publications, Harrisburg, PA., 1982

Weymouth, Lally, *Thomas Jefferson, The Man, His World, His Influence,* G.P. Putnam's Sons, New York, 1973

Whitehead, John W., *The Second American Revolution*, David C. Cook Publishing Co., Elgin, IL., 1982

Sun-tzu, *The Art of War*, (6th century, B.C.) Oxford University Press, New York, 1963

SEMINAR INFORMATION TEAR-OUT SHEET

If you are interested in learning more about our court system, or you presently are involved with a case against the IRS, then use this tear-out sheet to recieve more information about our seminar *Understanding Taxes and Court Procedure*. The information is free.

Understanding Taxes and Court Procedure has been taught to thousands of people all over the United States, and has helped them to solve their problems with the IRS. If you want to know more about how to help yourself, then do not hesitate to return this order form to us. When you send for more information, we will include a free copy of our **Tax Court Trouble-Shooting Guide**. This brochure has helped hundreds avoid the pitfalls inherent in a Tax Court case.

Photocopy this order form and mail it now

* * * * * * * * *

YES! I want more information about your seminar Understanding Taxes and Court Procedure. Include a free copy of the **Tax Court Trouble-Shooting Guide**.

Name _____

Address _____

City _____

State _____ Zip _____ Phone _____

Mail your order now. Our address is:
WINNING Seminars
506 Kenny Road, Suite 120
St. Paul, Minnesota 55101
612-774-0678

ABOUT THE AUTHOR

DANIEL J. PILLA — You've heard of him, about him, but not many know him. I do. Dan is a young, driven genius soon to have national recognition for his devoted effort to the restoration of Constitutional rights.

I am proud to have had the opportunity to work so closely with him. From him I have learned never to quit. As long as there is a heartbeat, there is hope.

His work over the past 10 years has been directed toward strengthening the heartbeat of the body of our country — the American citizen. A heartbeat that has been muffled by bureaucratic jibberish and concealment of the facts with legal and political jargon. Even the legal profession itself has come to recognize his ability to maneuver through the legal tax system and regularly calls upon him for assistance.

The one thing Dan has become most recognized for is his ability to teach the average person how to successfully defend himself in civil and criminal tax cases. He teaches people to be winners.

I am sure that after reading this book, you too will feel like you have won back some knowledge that perhaps has been hidden. As the attitude of the people becomes a winning attitude, the heartbeat of the nation will become stronger. Only with this strengthening can the power of "We the People" become a force to reckon with. I know you will enjoy this book!

Sincerely,

DAVID M. ENGSTROM

INFORMATION TEAR-OUT SHEET

FREE

Complimentary Issue of

Pilla Talks Taxes

A Newsletter that explores your rights and obligations with respect to the laws. Each information packed issue will feature articles on:

- IRS Procedure
- Deductions Under New Tax Laws
- Recent Court Decisions that will affect you
- Up-To-The Minute IRS Audit tips
- God's Law, Constitutional Law, Man's Law
- Hard Money Investments
- Social Insecurity Taxes

Each article will be written by recognized experts. This issue will give you ideas that can **Save You Money** and **Grief**. To receive your complimentary issue, fill out the information below and send this sheet to:

Name_____

Address_____

City _____

State_____ Zip_____ Phone _____

Mail your order now. Our address is:
WINNING Seminars
506 Kenny Road, Suite 120
St. Paul, Minnesota 55101
612-774-0678

NOTES

NOTES

NOTES

SEMINAR INFORMATION TEAR-OUT SHEET

If you are interested in learning more about our court system, or you presently are involved with a case against the IRS, then use this tear-out sheet to recieve more information about our seminar *Understanding Taxes and Court Procedure*. The information is free.

Understanding Taxes and Court Procedure has been taught to thousands of people all over the United States, and has helped them to solve their problems with the IRS. If you want to know more about how to help yourself, then do not hesitate to return this order form to us. When you send for more information, we will include a free copy of our **Tax Court Trouble-Shooting Guide**. This brochure has helped hundreds avoid the pitfalls inherent in a Tax Court case.

Photocopy this order form and mail it now

* * * * * * * * * *

YES! I want more information about your seminar Understanding Taxes and Court Procedure. Include a free copy of the Tax Court Trouble-Shooting Guide.

Name _____

Address _____

City _____

State _____ Zip _____ Phone _____

Mail your order now. Our address is:
WINNING Seminars
506 Kenny Road, Suite 120
St. Paul, Minnesota 55101
612-774-0678

SEMINAR INFORMATION TEAR-OUT SHEET

If you are interested in learning more about our court system, or you presently are involved with a case against the IRS, then use this tear-out sheet to recieve more information about our seminar *Understanding Taxes and Court Procedure*. The information is free.

Understanding Taxes and Court Procedure has been taught to thousands of people all over the United States, and has helped them to solve their problems with the IRS. If you want to know more about how to help yourself, then do not hesitate to return this order form to us. When you send for more information, we will include a free copy of our **Tax Court Trouble-Shooting Guide**. This brochure has helped hundreds avoid the pitfalls inherent in a Tax Court case.

Photocopy this order form and mail it now

* * * * * * * * * *

YES! **I want more information about your seminar Understanding Taxes and Court Procedure.** Include a free copy of the **Tax Court Trouble-Shooting Guide**.

Name _____

Address _____

City _____

State _____ Zip _____ Phone _____

Mail your order now. Our address is:
WINNING Seminars
506 Kenny Road, Suite 120
St. Paul, Minnesota 55101
612-774-0678

SEMINAR INFORMATION TEAR-OUT SHEET

If you are interested in learning more about our court system, or you presently are involved with a case against the IRS, then use this tear-out sheet to recieve more information about our seminar *Understanding Taxes and Court Procedure*. The information is free.

Understanding Taxes and Court Procedure has been taught to thousands of people all over the United States, and has helped them to solve their problems with the IRS. If you want to know more about how to help yourself, then do not hesitate to return this order form to us. When you send for more information, we will include a free copy of our **Tax Court Trouble-Shooting Guide**. This brochure has helped hundreds avoid the pitfalls inherent in a Tax Court case.

Photocopy this order form and mail it now

* * * * * * * * * *

YES! I want more information about your seminar Understanding Taxes and Court Procedure. Include a free copy of the **Tax Court Trouble-Shooting Guide**.

Name _____

Address _____

City _____

State _____ Zip _____ Phone _____

Mail your order now. Our address is:
WINNING Seminars
506 Kenny Road, Suite 120
St. Paul, Minnesota 55101
612-774-0678